Obsessed.

©2021 Karianne Gabaldon

All Rights Reserved

A poetry book about the struggles through a journey of mental illness.

1.

Afraid

I love it when I wake up and I forget how to breathe,
Asthmatic, a fanatic with the tricks inside my sleeve.
I guess that I'm a pest to everybody, guess I'll leave.
I don't wanna fucking leave,
I just wanna fucking grieve.
Uh.

They all say the road I'm going down will leave me
dead,
But is it so bad to wish that I never made this bed?
My life is going down the drain,
All I want to feel is pain,
Feel the downpour from the rain,
It is drenched inside the pane.

Okay, guess you've caught me, I am trying to escape,
I am sick and sad of sadness, it just tends to be my
fate.
And I'm here to tell you,
I won't compel you,
I wish you well, you.

Mama, can you save me?
I'm trapped inside a daydream.
I'm a lover undercover,
Never trust another.
I don't want to be,
Want to be afraid of me.

Save me,
I'm dying in a bad dream,
A nightmare at best.
I don't want to be,

Want to be afraid of me.

The truth inside here lies,
That I cannot hide my cries,
Please just do not sympathize,
I have had it with their lies.

I just want to know how one could really carry on,
How they know that something's wrong,
They all try to carry on.

I am over having catering to you,
I am all the stupid shit, the trauma I've been through.
I've reach the very drastic end,
Wanting to live life over, start again.
Knowing that it's wrong but I'll sin again,
Life is over and you cannot win.

2.

Here I am

I've stayed up endless nights,
Wondering why I'm this way.
People ask questions,
Something I live day by day.
Watching through windows,
Outside looks so easy, but I can't tell.

I'm puzzled by your ways,
Still can't keep up with you now.
They all think that I'm so strong,

But I gave my doctor a vow.
A vow that I'll never,
Stop trying to be better,
And that's a fact.
And this time you may rid me of all my damn selfish
acts.

Here I am;
I'm standing right under this Man,
I may believe in Him,
But not quite sure if he's the bad guy or good guy,
take my hand.
Here I am;
Please pray for me if you can,
I need a soft place to land.
Tear me apart, take the love from my heart.
But just understand,
Here I am.

Well I can't believe,
All of this poverty,
We reside.
I cannot wrap my around this world,
The brain of a sad girl,
Needs to hide.

Schizoaffective,
Obsessive Compulsive,
Look that shit up.
Then you'll see,
Why I am so hateful and torturing me,
I've lost every fuck.

Schizo, my heartache,
Your earthquake,
How you've burned me at the stake.
Dressed to impress,
But then make a big mess.
All the demons that I've seen,
That I've heard, are in me.
You've endangered my mind,
You've sewn my stitch in time.

But I took your needle before the thread came to an
end.
I've sewn up my patches on all your dispatches, oh
yeah.

Here I am;
I'm standing right under this Man,
I do believe in Him,
I'm still not sure if he's the good guy or bad guy,
Take my hand.
Here I am;
Please pray for me if you can,
I need a soft place to land.
Tear me apart, take the love from my heart.
But just understand,
Here I am.

Too Bad, Too Bad

You and I now again collide.
You have beaten my insides,
Can't quite count the tears I've cried.
I need that card that you haven't handed,
Your little smile so cheesy, candid,
You've left me deserted on an isle, stranded.

Whoa, I'm taking it in,
Whoa where do I begin?
Leave me, leave me with this sin.

Too bad, too bad, I've given up.
I thought that you and I were once,
Friend inside of me, you try to hide from me, love.
It was us.
Too bad, too bad, I've given up.
My brain, my conscience is so fucked,
I made a bed I can't get out of, so what?
Leave me here with my schizophrenia.

Might as well be on your side.
Gotta swallow my shit pride,
Nowhere to run, nowhere to hide.
No one here to save me now,
All my friends have me so down,

Their knife-like fingers, here I drown.

Whoa, I'm taking it in,
Whoa, I'm high again.
Schizophrenia, I've let you win.
4.

Addiction

I relapsed;
The scars on my arm prove my past,
Can't haunt me forever.
A flashback,
Leaving it all up to the flask,
In his hand, my endeavor,
Is to live and let die, let go.
I'm stuck in the snow.
Unstoppable, they say,
But in reality, I just want to cave.
I want to drag myself to fear,
I want to haunt my childhood years.
All this mourning has got me wishing,
That I could be one with my addiction.

5.

Here

It's time that I left you alone,
Please go find your way back home,
I need to reignite my lovely fire.
The heart inside me burns like hell,
And yours is cold and I can tell,
That you've just dried up my wishing well.
The things you do to me are not okay,

But I think I like your doing anyway.

So this is where I come back to you,
This is is where I stop feeling blue.
I need you here, I need you here.
I know I said I don't want you back,
But without you I'm off my fast track.
I need you here, I need you here.

If only I'd known who you were,
I wouldn't think you're better off with her,
Your voice inside my head still drives me nuts.
And I feel like I've just been used,
But you're like my drug, I have to use,
Just stay above the heavy love.

I need you here.
You're my worst fear.
I need you here.

6.

Antibiotic

I said I need a brand new man,

One that likes you, one than can,
Ignite my fire.
Then the stars stop spangling,
And you leave me dangling,
On a tight wire.

Because we do what we should not,
We don't live by the way we're taught,
We live free.
But I really believed in you,
Believed in all the things you do,
You were right for me.

Change this story, turn it around,
But you know you'll only hear the sound,
Of my screaming antics.
So I just rid you,
Get my fix, too,
Antibiotic.

I was surprised when you looked perplexed,
When I said that I wasn't looking for sex,
You paid that bill.
When you first wrote me, I smiled,
When the second of your face had me beguiled,
That time stood still.

You're gone now and to get rid of you,
To get out my mind, stop feeling blue,
I take this pill...
I take the pill and it eases my mind,
And I feel like I might get better in time,
It's my free will...

So I just rid you,
Get my fix, too,
Antibiotic.

7.

A Soft Place To Land

Hey there, Sunday,
How've you been? I've missed you.
I've been okay,
Tough times I have been through.
Infatuations I have don't last very long,
I look to the right but I'm always wrong.
Dirty crosses, filthy runs among.

And I'm just biting my tongue,
Wishful thinking that they'll change, they're just too
young.
And I just do not understand,
The bottle's broken, I've got glass in my hand,
I just want a man,

A soft place to land.

Hey there, Monday,
I will have arrived soon.
Hoping someday,
I'll stop being a loon.
Maybe if I'm not crazy, guys will come around,
Tiptoes on my heartbeat, screaming sounds.
Maybe that's why crazy's not allowed.

And I'm just biting my tongue,
Wishing that I could just stay forever young.
And it's hard to understand,
Why nobody's gonna hold my hand,
Just really need a soft place to land.

Count my pennies in a jar,
Send overdrive in my heart.
Sometimes wrecking my car,
Is so that I can find peace in life.
I'll just find a new release,
A new way to finally please.
Just want life to be at ease,
Without using the edge of my knife.

And in my sweet dreams,
You're in my mind.
It's not what it seems,
It's such my life.
It's absurd,
You have my word.

And I was biting my tongue,

Keeping my head held high, my hammock well hung.
And I'm lying down now,
Praying to God that maybe somehow…

And I was biting my tongue,
Finally at peace, breathing right out of my lungs.
I wish I could understand,
But it's okay, someday I'll find a man,
He will finally hold my hand,
A soft place to land.

Kari, Throw The Razor Away

The remorse said it best,
That the stains on your dress,
Have yet to be polished off.
You've appeared from nowhere,
You've even cut your own hair,
You've changed, but nobody cares.

Oh, your insides,
Eat you every time that you want to die.
You're coming back for more.

Is it time yet?
Catching your death?
Kari, throw the razor away.
The blade ain't worth it,
All of the bullshit,
That you had done before will haunt you in the future
someday.

And the blood on your arm,
Though it's doing you harm,
You need to find a new fix.
'Cause the cockroaches will,
Torture you until they're killed,
You know it's always like this.

Oh, your own faith,
Is measured by the way you see your face,

And here comes the downpour.

Don't you want to go back again,
Back in time, remember when,
Life wasn't so hard.
And when you look upon your sad days,
You will find better ways,
Just trust in your heart.

All you had done before will haunt you in the future
someday...

9.

Please Cry, Olivia.

Olivia, please answer the door,
Your insides are fading to the core,
But instead you starve yourself for more.
Baby, I just know you're in there,
I know that here and you're aware,
I want you know that I still do care.

Why aren't you crying,
I see you dying,

Bloodstains on my floor.
Between the razor and our savior,
That you choose to ignore.
I'll save your life,
Please just put down the knife.
Your heart is mine to have and to hold.

Olivia, why don't you answer?
This shit just keeps on eating like cancer,
I want you, just move on, my dancer.
Oh, my honey, you are too beautiful,
You do not see it when you look,
Inside the mirror, you are hooked.

You don't need a reason why your ways,
Crumble up inside you every day.
You don't want to know what I go through,
Just being worried about you.

Satin Sheets

I was a lonesome dove,
Falling for fiction love,
Drowning in my own suds,
I just could not keep up.

Then when my mom said enough,
I took my boxing gloves,
Tired and all fed up,
I thought I knew love...

But I was wrong,
Satin sheets,
Don't belong,
In the streets.

Where I am,
King size bed,
Now I'm home.
Resting my head.

Looking back as a child,
Running endlessly wild,
Hoping to be someday,
Someone big that gets paid.

There are so many words,
I can say but it hurts,
So I just use my pen,
Scribble down what goes first.

I'm in a castle now,
Fit for a queen somehow,
I am just so in awe,
Finally took that vow.

Of many books I write,
Telling them day and night,
Staring at starry moons,
It will just not suffice.

11

Where Have You Gone?

You said someday that we may meet,
But now I might just choose defeat,
Lay my armor down right by my feet.

Our love it cannot be ignored,
You shut me out then slam the door,

You dry my drought and flood my downpour.

In your eyes I'm probably dead to you,
But to you I just cannot refuse,
To tell you that it's you that I can't lose.

And this is it, I'm standing here now,
Knocking at your door, but you're out.
Where have you gone?
Where have you gone?

I need your honest eyes today,
Do you really mean what you say?
Where have you gone?
Where have you gone?

My heart it tells me to ignore,
All the feelings that are unsure,
Is it true, am I that of a bore?

Before you left with her, your heart was true,
Now yours is red and mine is blue,
I want you in my life, I just can't lose you.

And then that silly feeling sinks in,
I think of that insatiable kiss.
Where have you gone?
Where have you gone?

My mother, should have listened to her,
I should have been much smarter, wiser.
Where have you gone?
Where have you gone?

12.

The Pleasure Is Treasure

Anticipation sets my mind,
Smooth his skin and not a wrinkle in time,
An accidental tongue slip embraces my pearly whites,
Pearly whites.

And now I'm watching him as he devours me,
I have been locked in, he has the key.
He opens me up with the lock now,
And he goes down...

The pleasure is treasure, mmm,
I'm cannot stop this,
It's mad, mad, mad.
I am falling in love,
Every touch of your kiss,
Drives me mad, mad, mad.
You're the best I've ever had.

Fluttering with butterflies,
Monarch cocoons,
As I swoon,
Find forbidden love under an unfamiliar moon,

We dance in the sheets all afternoon.

And I'm about to break and collapse,
But then he takes it to the max,
I moan out of my thorax,
Then we both climax.

Let's go explore space,
Rev the rocket, rev the rocket.
Let's get out of this place,
Rev the rocket, rev the rocket.

You're the best I've ever had.

13.

Don't Worry

You just kill me with your fire,
Have me walking a tight wire.
You prey on me so nervously,
You couldn't fall in love with me.
And the hurtful things you say,
They will haunt us both someday.
You stare into the hourglass,
Hoping that my time will pass.

You just say I'm headed straight for doom.
Don't worry,

Don't worry,
I'll be gone soon.
Mark my words, I'll leave this crowded room.
Don't worry,
Don't worry,
I'll be gone soon.

I still remember when we wed,
You called me awful names in bed.
You just felt like the dominant,
I tried to call for self defense.

But after all those years have gone,
I still feel I'm in the wrong.
Are you seeing what you did to me?
Guess it's just my turn to leave.
I am over you,
Don't worry, we're through.
I'm done being blue,
I'll find somebody new.
Go fuck yourself, too.

14.

Dancing In The Sheets

I'll be your first time,
You'll be my last time, darling.
The way you look at my face,

Your eyes, colors are now shapes.
Your head,
My bed.
We'll take it so slow.
We will get through long distance somehow,
But now that you're here, let's just make love now.

Dancing in the sheets with you,
Darling, it's what I wanna do.
I wanna taste your essence,
I hunger for your fluorescent.
Dancing in the sheets all night,
Baby, all I can do is cry.
I'm happy that you're with me,
So how about we dance in the sheets?

I promise I won't hurt you,
Please just be honest if I do.
Discover you while kissing,
I want to be what you're missing.
This man,
My hand,
We'll someday make it.
But darling, just relax, I'm happy here.
Now that you're with me, let's make love, dear.
I'll be your first time,
You'll be my last time, darling.

15.

Ain't No Rest For The Writers (A Cage The Elephant Parody Poem)

There was a time where I,
Just sat and cried,
From the fact I got such a bad review.
I wanted to give up,
I had pressed my luck,
I closed my laptop, I was through.

But then I rewind to,
Where I left you,
Down and low, so heavy and dry.
And I write it down,
And then my frown,
Turns into a happy smile.

You know there ain't no rest for the writers,
Writing don't come at ease,
We've got bills to pay, we've got mouths to feed,
And it might bring you on your knees.

You think it pays so well,

Maybe down in hell,
Though I sure wish it did.
You know there ain't no rest for the writers,
But the writers don't give a shit.

I think that someday I'll give in,
But I really wanna win,
This contest that's for story of the year.
I just might show down,
All of these clowns,
Who like to live in utter fear.

I'll write chapter one,
And I am done,
As long you know I have written it for you.
And I'll tell you why,
I made you die,
In my story, yeah, here's the truth.

I woke up last night,
After a fight,
With a head, I fell to my knees.
I said, "hey, might as well,
Make this a story to tell",
So I put my fingers on the keys.

I wrote about what it'd be like,
To be a guy named Mike,
Where he lived in a white gold house.
And then Mike went, offed himself,
I placed the story on a shelf,
Then I stopped writing, lighting I did douse.

You think it pays so well,
Maybe down in hell,
Though I sure wish it did.
You know there ain't no rest for the writers,
But the writers don't give a shit.

16.

Quicksand

Self sabotaging, here I will stay,
Letting go, I drown myself.
Hold the railing, but I fall anyway,
Don't ever say I never asked for help.
And now,
I can't control anymore,
I can't stop creaking the floors,

You shut my exit doors,
As I burn the sun.

The one true friend I once had,
She's hooked on razors, Prozac,
And now I'm under attack,
Think that I am done.
My endless sadness, madness falls through,
I tried to hide it all.
There's nobody I can really talk to,
So a downward spiral I fall.

Oh, mother dearest, sorry,
Your daughter's fine, don't worry,
She's just a little dirty,
She will sleep tonight.
It seems to always happen,
I escaped the insane pen,
Want to know where I have been?
Won't give you a fright.

The pain I feel is evergreen,
I reach inside me, pull the string.
Then once I've fallen down to,
The spot in my heart I left off to.
I want to show them all my love,
Want to show that I'm above,
My self injury,
But into me,
You'll never fall.

Fourteen years now, fourteen too late,
I thought I was ready to choose my fate.

Turned out to just be a day,
That I woke up and I'm not okay.
I would've been so great to you,
What a shame I'm crazy as hell,
Oh well.
I had you under my spell,
Now I'm underground in hell.

I can't believe it happened,
This day is ever saddened,
I don't know why you'd come back,
So I understand.
This is my final entry,
I promise I won't kill me,
You've done it all already,
Sunken quicksand.
Forever here I will be,
Down in quicksand.

17.

Hydroplaned Plane

Booked a flight for 7 in the morn,
Had enough, started to feel a little worn.
There's too much chaos going on in my head,
There's too much places that I've never fled.
So tired, yeah, I couldn't stay awake,
I'm still here to make more mistakes.
Better run, better get on my plane,
So I can run away and not deal with the pain.
My love, my life,
Is dead and dry,
It's time to head up to the sky.
Sun is up and I'm ready to fly.

Hydroplaned Plane crashing in the sky,
Off the runway, what a wild ride.
We lifted off but stopped, heading nowhere,
Instead we're mentally and physically impaired.
My whole thoughts have turned into half walls,
Giving up, done going through with it all.
A cry for help won't do any good,

So I just board like a good girl should.
The plane it plans to get off at a spot,
Tonight I'm leaving with an empty slot.
Now the rain's coming, pouring down my face,
I drown in the water, tears won't be replaced.

And you may think I'm ready now,
To leave this world, I don't know how.
I just don't want to say goodbye.

Show my ticket to the stewardess,
Have my empty luggage claimed on this,
Plane I think I'll be content to ride,
Lonely for so long, don't need one by my side.
I get on board and I fasten my seat,
Ask the stewardess for a treat.
The the plane takes off to fly,
I am ready, I can't deny.
Hydroplaned Plane crashing in the sky,
Off the runway, what a wild ride.
We lifted off but stopped, heading nowhere,
Instead we're mentally and physically impaired.

18.

Charcoal

So many thoughts inside my head,
The tap has shut off, I feel so dead.
Could it be,

Am I fading?
Walk away from the fire alarm,
Turned to soot from charcoal heart.
My time's come,
All alone.

My only station is dehydration,
Need a vacation, my mind is racing.
Cluttered desk,
I'll sleep peacefully when at rest.
Oh God I'm just such a mess…
Here's the drought, I have drained the sea.
No one knows what's going on with me.
Therapy,
No one cares, don't you see.

Shed some light on a darkened thing,
Crimson love, self hate glistening.
I'm dead to me,
Everyone else agrees.
Tell me where to go,
My heart's burnt out, you know.
My smile is deranged, eyes they don't glow.
Want to be someone different in life,
Someone I'll never show.

This Is Just A Test...

Send me off to sleep,
Shut my dizzy eyes,
Hinder all my voices,
So they never realize,

All the things that hunt me,
My mind has gone astray,
Will strike the clock at midnight,
I'll leave my slipper, run away.
I need some time to think about my well-being,
If you just knew all of the things that I've seen,
Oh, they you would not leave me dry and breathless,
I think I'll pass as I must go fail this test.

Darkness has arrived,
I'm out on my own,
Prince Charming isn't here yet,
Oh, I feel so alone.
Oh, I have felt this freedom,
In my mind way too long,
Thinking I'm a free bird,
But forgot the cuckoo song.

All my hopes and dreams,
Are buried in a ditch.
Razor, stay away from me,

You'll never,
You'll never know what you'll catch.
What you'll catch...
Oh, you'll catch...

20.

Ultraviolet

There I was all cornered up,
Twisted mind, shit out of luck,
Thought they were all after me.
Momma, daddy, baby sis,
I just threw a major fit,
Thinking all unnaturally.

Now I can see the light,
Ultraviolet.
I can see the light,
Ultraviolet.
This supernova crashes into me,
I'm suddenly sparked up, landing in the sea.
My endless dreamer,
It is you and me.
The light is ultraviolet.

So I lie back in the chair,

Thinking what is hard to bear.
Just relax, enjoy the breeze.
Hear the owls, like oh, my my.
Not a cloud up in the sky,
Feel the wind, now I'm at peace.
Now I can see the light,
Ultraviolet.

I can see the light,
Ultraviolet.
Please don't go away, my music box.
Please don't shine away my lifelong dreams.
Please don't go away, my music box,
Please don't shine away my lifelong dreams.

21.

My Deadly Desire

I'm hungry for hurt,
Desperate for death,
Little do they know I'm wasting every breath.

I want someone to realize,
But then again I don't.
I want someone to hear my cries but do something,
they won't.

It's not attention,
It's for thrill,
I'm not a killer I just like to be killed.

I don't do it on purpose,
I do it for purpose.
I want to feel, scream, lose myself in a circus.

Deadly daydreams are chasing me,
Noble knives aren't fazing me,
I need to feel something, I need not to breathe.

I've become a monster;
A frail foe, you see.
My deadly desire, what have you done to me?

22.

I Can't

My bath water runs dry,
Here comes the drought.
I think it's safe to say that there is no way out.
I think the side effects are flaring up now,
But you wouldn't know,
Missus "holier than thou".

Oh, I had a way of shining,
But you stole my shine.
After all, I'd say sorry for wasting your time.
And even thought you excused my,
Cellophane lies,
I had still walked that invisible thin line.

But I'm here to say,
That I won't need you anyway.
Guess I should use you,
The way you used me, hey…

I'm flying solo like Hans who fought the wars,
Silent but deadliest of the many little whores,
I can't tell,
Wish you well,
And I'd forget about it,
But I can't.

My tears are stained glass,
On my swollen, soft cheek.
And here I lie standing, both mild and meek.
I think the ceiling has yet another leak,

It's been pouring down,
Like rain in the street.

You're so stuck on your sickness,
You can't focus on mine.
But believe me, I know that you're more sick,
I hear it all the time.
I can't breathe,
And you see,
I'd forget about it,
But I can't.

Yeah, my family tree has missing limbs,
Struck by lightning.
Oh, believe it, come on tell me I'm not right,
Fucked in the head,
Soul is dead,
I'd forget about it,
But I can't.

Clock strikes one and I'm here all alone,
I guess I'm the stranger walking the little girl home,
Guess I'm not the victim, no not anymore,
Guess I'll pack up my things and I'll walk out the
door...

But one more thing before I drift off to sleep,
Your secrets are my alibis,
To them I will keep.
You're so oblivious,
And it's marvelous,
Oh, I can't...

23.

Consent

My body bleeds your name;
Unfamiliar poison.
I'll go and keep your word,
While you keep my skirt.

I look at the sunset,
Reminding me of sunrise,
Just this morning was,
An endless nightfall.

So if you need me,
I'll be bruised and battered,
Like a fried fish in a tavern...

You need to know,
I was alone.
I was vulnerable, too late,
And you stole my smile off my face.
Robbery at best,
Take the rest.
And fuck you too,
But my consent,
Costs too much to pay the rent.

It costed too much wasted,
Just like your guilty conscience.
I guess that I will just laugh,
Instead of feeling haunted.

I guess next time that I see you,
Won't be that so sweet, huh?
Maybe next time we meet,
I'll stand my damn guard.

So if you need me,
I'll be bruised and battered,
Like a fried fish in a tavern...

You need to know,
I was alone.
I was vulnerable, too late,
And you stole my smile off my face.
Robbery at best,

Take the rest.
And fuck you too,
But my consent,
Costs too much to pay the rent.

I am here to remind you,
That mind's in your zipper,
I'll give you time,
You can give me back my skirt…
And you can take back your word…

You need to know,
I was alone.
I was vulnerable, too late,
And you stole my smile off my face.
Robbery at best,
Take the rest.
And fuck you too,
But my consent,
Costs too much to pay the rent.

You need to know,
I was alone.
I was vulnerable, too late,
And you stole my smile off my face.
Robbery at best,
Take the rest.
And fuck you too,
But my consent,
Costs too much to pay the rent.

24.

Chardonnay Glass

Nobody knows you like I thought I knew you,
Your Cheshire Cat smile, my awakening was rude,
I wish I could take back all that I've said,
It's time for you to get the hell out of my head.
Wasted days and wasted nights,
I win this fight.

Your plan went well, but you knew already,
But your even flow is kind of unsteady.
I'll never know,
Why you had to go,

A little off your rocker, aren't you?
You may have had them fooled, but I know,
Because of you,
I have a different view.

Sitting at the Omni, saying that you want me,
Giving up the hope that I'll end up in your arms,
But then you pull me in.

I cannot recall a day I didn't bawl,
I never thought of you as a man who'd end it all,
But I thought wrong.
And all along...
You have me twisted like your whiskey and Coke,

The way you fooled me was no joke,
But I am finding new ways to cope,
Cope.
I couldn't see through those damn eyes,
Or waking up to you during sunrise,
Now I just want you out of my life.
Life.

25.

Filthy Is Not A Cry For Help

Listen to Hitchcock's crows sing,
Wait for the dirty bells to ring,
Inside that chapel lies a filthy whore,
I'll take all of my dignity while I close the door.

He hasn't any idea how much,
I've missed his kiss, in dire of his touch.
As she walks down the floral aisle,
She puts on a fake, plastered smile.

And wow!
There it goes, all of it,
All we had has turned to shit.
She's not gonna get away with it...

No... no... she won't get away with it.

Dirty!
What they'll say when they find out.
Sleazy!
What they'll call her without a doubt.
Slutty!
They will yell when they find out she cheats.
Ooh, boy, are they in for a treat!
(Guess that I'll just wait,
I'll see how it plays out.
Guess that I'll just wait,
I'll see how it plays out.)

Dear groom, if I may, can I make a toast?
I'd love to see your marriage up in flames and roast.
She will never do to you what I do well,
So fuck this marriage, she can rot in hell!

As I watch the reception,
Burn to utter perfection,
He stares right at me,
With a smile from cheek to cheek.

Ooh, how he grins with his teeth,
How he rushes up to hold me.
How the whore stares me down...
Yeah, I'm actually really enjoying this now.

Filthy is not a cry for help.
Filthy is not a cry for help.
Filthy is not a cry for help.
Filthy is not a cry for help.

26.

Crazy Camp

I see them making funny faces,
While I'm in my darkest places,
Feels like all I ever do is race to lose.
Nurse comes in, evaluates me,
Checks my every injury,
As I secretly look around for clues.

I think that I've been here before,
This place is so haunting,
I'm not at home not anymore,
All I get is taunting, oh.

My mind has gone awry;
It has been wrung out, ever dry.
I think that I've been here before…

So I flee into the day room,
Daddy calls, says I'll be out soon,
Momma wants me to wait a couple weeks.

I say, "I can't really, momma",
Because I won't face the trauma,
This place has given me PTSD.

I think that I've been here before,
This place is so haunting,
I'm not at home not anymore,
All I get is taunting, oh.

My mind has gone awry;
It has been wrung out, ever dry.
I think that I've been here before…

The doctors in,
This time it ends,
Explain to him all my issues.
Can't believe,
He's making me stay more weeks,
I'm always on the losing streak.
With a flushed look on my cheek,
I just want to go home,
Want to go home.
Want to go home.
I just want to go home.

I think that I've been here before,
This place is so haunting,
I'm not at home not anymore,
All I get is taunting, oh.

My mind has gone awry;
It has been wrung out, ever dry.
I think that I've been here before…

The doctors in,
This time it ends,
Explain to him all my issues.
Can't believe,
He's making me stay more weeks,
I'm always on the losing streak.
With a flushed look on my cheek,
I just want to go home.

27.

You Did This

Look inside the mirror,
What ghost have we here?
I'm dead and forgotten,
It's never been so clear.

Locked inside a lions cage,
Fighting my way out.
Bruised and battered, filled up with rage,
To live, I highly doubt.

Oh, you did this,
You sang upon my sorrows.
Oh, I feel like shit,

I don't see a tomorrow.
Oh, you throw a fit,
And you leave me here hollow.
Oh, you did this,
You sang upon my sorrows.

And my day is done,
Your dark shadow will come.
Haunting me frantically,
Oh, the damage is all done.

Oh, locked inside a prison,
The only renegade.
Fighting for redemption,
Fighting to be saved.

Oh, you did this,
You sang upon my sorrows.
Oh, I feel like shit,
I don't see a tomorrow.
Oh, you throw a fit,
And you leave me here hollow.
Oh, you did this,
You sang upon my sorrows.

You sang upon my sorrows...
You sang upon my sorrows...
Everything went black,
It's suddenly unclear.
Where did my sunlight shine to?
It's gone,
It's gone, it's never coming back.
Coming back,

Never coming back.

Oh, you did this,
You sang upon my sorrows.
Oh, I feel like shit,
I don't see a tomorrow.
Oh, you throw a fit,
And you leave me here hollow.
Oh, you did this,
You sang upon my sorrows.

28.

I Want You

She has a frozen heart;
Too gentle, too fragile,
I brought her to her knees,
She swore she was docile.

But baby needs a new game;
She's wicked, she's evil.
And now I'll never be the same,
The poison set in me.

I take her up on her bargain,
Give in to her plea.
But now I'm someone different,
What's happened to me?

What does she expect?
Does she expect me to just bow down?
I feel the darkness,
Here comes the showdown.

She's looking at me,
What do I do?
She reminds me of Uncle Sam,
Saying "I Want You!"

Baby has a taste for vengeance,
A passion for crime.
Her backgammon is ruthless,
Guess I ran out of time.

I take her up on her bargain,
Give in to her plea.
But now I'm someone different,
What's happened to me?

29.

I Thought

I'm sitting here on a wooden floor,
Just praying for my life.
Don't know whether to call my mom,
The words cut like a knife.
You were one thing I was sure about,

The one thing I could trust.
But then those slaughter words you yelled at me call
it filthy lust.

I am shaking, tears are tumbling down,
Like tumbleweeds in heat.
There are kids sleeping away softly,
As your mouth dances in the street.
Acting gangster, acting tough,
I've never seen this side of you.
And to think we had what we once had,
To me, you won't be true.

Thought I was wrong,
Thought I deserved it.
Thought I was capable of doing on my own.
Thought all along,
That's your scarf I knitted.
Thought I would get the love I've shown.

The bottle seems to drown your tears,
But it's gone what else will you do?
I wish I could erase the years,
And all the shit you put me through.
In your own way you were nice to me,
This I'll never, ever doubt.
But with all that is left of me,
I'm gonna see my way out.

We were close enough to fly away,
Together in the end.
But now my angel she is gone today,
You've found a new best friend.

I won't ever mentioned how you hurt me so,
I'll never let you in.
I'll just lie here on this hard, cold floor,
While you live in sin.

And with my hurt heart I'll just smile, wave goodbye,
Wishing you hadn't left me but,
Moving on I have to try.
And I'm likely to have moved by now,
But you just can't see that I need you in my life
somehow.

And you're not who I used to anymore,
It's funny liquor can open your mouth but close a lot
of doors.
So I get up off the hard wooden floor.

30.

Autoimmune

Want to take the pain away from you just like
morphine,
You act like it is nothing, I cannot believe what I've
seen.
I love the fact that you're always on me for what I do,
Because you're loving me just like I adore you.

Your inspiration's kept me from eternal hell,
My fate has gone away and I have all to tell.
I'll gladly take the bullet if it comes to this,
I'm sorry that you have to feel like shit.

It's alright, stay here,
I need you.
I'm right here and I love you too.
Every ounce of pain,
Fills rivers like the rain.

And I see the bravery,
You hold tight.
You keep me going, my smile shining bright.
But mom you have my heart,
Don't you dare depart.

Don't think that I don't notice when you're feeling hurt,
Don't think that I don't notice when you're at your worst.
I'll suck out all of your poison with my syringe,
To me it kind of looks like your door is unhinged.

I hope that this is the worst that it ever gets,
You've taught me some life lessons I'll never forget.
I love you so damn much sometimes it hurts inside,
And it hurts me everyday to see your sad eyes cry.

I'm sorry that it ends this way,
I'm sorry that you won't get back,
Everything that you once had wanted,
Now you are haunted by a blood fiend gnat.

I guess your love is all I need,
To make it through all my tough days,
I guess that even though you smile it'll take awhile to hide all your cries.

Lord lay your hands on the girl,
After all she is my whole world,
Someday you'll get to find your pearl.

Want to take the pain away from you just like
morphine,
You act like it is nothing, I cannot believe what I've
seen.

Unstable

I'm sitting here with voices in my head,
I can't quite remember what you've said.
I need another break away from you,
And the stupid shit you do.
My mental state is debilitating,
It's so hard and frustrating.
I know you try your hardest,
But that's the whole damn purpose.

You didn't do a thing to upset me
(I'm just unstable, you see),
You heart will always hold my key
(I'm just unstable, you see).

It will last forever, my sickness.
But I won't miss our first kiss.
You didn't do a thing to upset me
(I'm just unstable, you see).

It'll all just crumble down on me,
When you come along then you will see.
That the same effect won't be the cause,
Now if you'll hold the applause.
My voices are already clapping now,
You can't hear them, but somehow,
You have every right to be mad,
'Cause of the love that we once had.

Just let me go back to where I once was,
I'll better up then we'll have our buzz.
You'll get drunk off me,
I'll get drunk of you...
Just like we always used to do...
32.

Mentally Drained

Dark clouds rolling in,
The sky fades to black.
Looks like we are finished,
There's no turning back.

All the love I've given away,
All my bridges break.
I feel like I'm obliged to stay,
Don't know if I can take.

Oh, we're mentally,
Drained and we are drowning.
Oh, especially,
Our smiles to frowning.
Oh, we're broken, we,
Are saving up for crowning.
Oh, we're mentally,
Drained and we are drowning.

People don't know why,
We do what we do.

They're always asking questions,
Feel like I am through.

Wakes you up at midnight,
The visions and the screams.
Howling at the moonlight,
Destroying all your dreams.

Oh, we're mentally,
Drained and we are drowning.
Oh, especially,
Our smiles to frowning.
Oh, we're broken, we,
Are saving up for crowning.
Oh, we're mentally,
Drained and we are drowning.

I feel eyes on me,
They're watching every move.
Then I wake and I see,
Sunlight in the moon.

The moon…
Oh, the moon.

33.

Crystal

The mess I've made was awful bloody,
And I won't tell anybody,
I just wanted to be somebody to you.
If I died, would you have noticed?
Would have been depressed or pissed?
Would desolation crave you in your room?

I think you miss me all too much,
You just haven't said the words yet.
My smell, my kiss, my words, my touch,
It still drives you crazy, yes.
I was your home,
Now you're sleeping in bed alone.
I think you miss me all too much.

Was it worth it kissing Crystal?
Was she happy, ever blissful?
Did it taste like sugar cookie, her kiss?
Crystal I think had it coming,
She had a face that's awful numbing,
That made you come back running to this.

I think you miss me all too much,
And you know I already know.
Our relationship patch was rough,
So you threw it the window.
Back in high school,
Back behind Wal Mart, we were cool.
I think you miss me all too much

So Crystal's gone.
Forsooth anon,
You'll be back in my arms again.

I grabbed the rifle, I was done,
You didn't even hear the gun.
And I think I've become,
Your someone.

I think you've missed me all too much,
And baby now we're happy.
I've finally sewn this rough patch up,
You'll never ever be lonely.
Second guessed times,
Back whenever I had never called you mine.
I think you've missed me all too much.

34.

Freezing Cold

Here, I'm stranded,
Lying in the sands of doubt,
No way out.
Strangling sadness,
Constricted madness.
Take my life,
I've already tried.

"Rise above the drastic,"
They say.
But how am I when plastic's
At play.
Puppies purring,
Kittens scurrying.
Be afraid,

For today.

And I was skating the truth,
Down a rusty half pipe,
Fell in the fountain of youth.
And though I'm growing so old,
My mental state will leave me so,
Freezing cold.
Dirty vengeance,
Crispy conscience,
Telling me,
Who I should be.

It's never worth it,
But I dived dirty.
Was a saint,
Now I'm drained.
All my bluest skies are now turned grey,
You should watch out when I'm at play.
I've caused the damage,
And I can't stand it.
Mental health,
Not myself.

And I was skating the truth,
Down a rusty half pipe,
Fell in the fountain of youth.
And though I'm growing so old,
My mental state will leave me so,
Freezing cold.

Caught in heavy, raging storms,
Trying to keep myself warm.

But always letting me down,
Schizo psycho lives in town.
...and I frown...
...they look down...

And I was riding my skates,
Rolling down the rink,
It's been a very tough day.
And though I'm growing so old,
My mental state will leave me so,
Freezing cold.
Freezing cold...
My mental state will leave me so,
Freezing cold...

Confidant

There I was just sitting there,
Listening to Hip To Be Scared,
Ice Nine Kills our favorite band.
I know I'll never be the same,
Laughter, smiling, no head games,
No longer deep in the sand.

And I can say for a fact,
You're my confidant.

May have known you for a bit,
But the rest don't give a shit,
You were nice when no one was.
And now they're dying to be friends,
Ain't that always how it ends?
Fighting over me like cubs.

But they're not my confidant.
You're my confidant.

I can tell you anything I want,
Nightmares, daydreams,
I trust you with my heart.
Thank you for listening,
To each every part,
You are my confidant.

I may not know you that well…

Please don't go away, my confidant.

Please don't find somewhere else to go.
Please don't go away, my confidant.
Please don't find somewhere else to go.

36.

Sprinkler

I have something to say,
About two nights ago,
When you made your escape,
I bet you didn't know,
That I wept.
Wept... wept... wept, wept.

But then, of course you did,
Go and tell your friends,
About the stupid shit,
That just doesn't make sense.
Your ship wrecked.
Shipwreck... shipwreck... wreck, wreck.

And I know it's all,
A game to you.
But I know now,
There's nothing I can do.

'Cause now you're standing out in my front lawn,

You want me back.
You're begging on your knees, I yawn,
Because we fell off track,
Oh.

You are outside standing on my front lawn,
You want me back.
It was your fault I moved on.

A little birdie said,
Your loving ain't the same.
I'm not fucked in the head,
But I'm fucked in the brain.
What's your deal,
Your deal... your deal... deal, deal.

I think it's over now,
I think I'm gonna go.
But then you hold back,
And say to me, "oh, no."
You don't feel,
Don't feel... don't feel... feel, feel.

And it's just all,
A game to you.
You keep coming back,
What the hell am I do?

When the waterworks,
Come sprinkling out.
Maybe then you'll realize,
It's over now,
It's over now...

It over... now.

37.

Completely

My days were as cold as the lakes in the winter,
My darkness so dark that the color went tinted.
The midsummer night's dream was only a nightmare,
I grew up so fast that it gave me a scare...

I don't wanna grow up,
Knowing that I grew without you.
I don't wanna show up,
At your your doorstep, calling out for you.
I just want you right here, right now,
With me.
We'll be completely,
Only completely.

I made a mistake just by letting you leave me,
Watching you go was such a crash.
You wounded my heart by a cardiac slaughter,
Your feelings, though, gave me whiplash.
Maybe you fell in love with some other girl,
Maybe you casted a spell, suddenly were her world.
Maybe I'll never be the same without ballgown twirl.
I was your girl.
Oh.

You're only my completely,
Completely,
Completely,
Completely.
You're only completely,
Completely,
Completely,
Completely.

And I just wish that it was
(Goodbye love),
Different, and you meant
(Oh my God above),

Your love was mine, all the time
(I just need your love).
Now I'm broken
(Broken).

And I just want you tonight
(But it's too late now),
Being here, hold me tight
(Oh, but somehow)
The black of night, my starry eyes
(Coyotes on the prowl).
Now I'm broken.

Completely.
Completely,
I wanna be yours,
Completely.
I don't wanna grow up,
Knowing that I grew without you.
I don't wanna show up,
At your your doorstep, calling out for you.
I just want you right here, right now,
With me.
We'll be completely,
Only completely.

38.

Hard To Bear

Pleasure, pain,
Love and lust.
Deeply shallow,
Beauty is hideous.

Your terrible,
Is my conceit.
My guilty pleasure,
But I crossed defeat.

I rest my head on the black pavement.
I think I'm dead, is this what you meant,
When your lips read I am next.
I want to wear your face, wear your hex.

A stranger's home is where I reside,
Can't quite see the truth in lies,

I'm so naive,
Yeah, I just want to die.

Agony haunts my twisted, fucked up brain,
But you just don't care.
You make it hard to bear.
A fear of being nothing,
I want to be something.
But you just don't care.
You make it hard to bear,
You make it hard to bear.

Caved in caverns, I stand tall,
I just want to say fuck it all.
My shallow breath I try to hide,
But my strongest suit starts to die.
Your pillow talk,
Your stolen crown.
I won it all,
Yet you take me down.

A stranger's home is where I reside,
Can't quite see the truth in lies,
I'm so naive,
Yeah, I just want to die.

Want the world to see,
Who you are so they'll believe me.
And your majesty,
I have no choice, I have to obey thee.
You are me...

Drought

Exercise;
The fluids run their course.
Nobody knows,
About my sealed-shut drawers.
So many secrets,
I have kept inside.
The water flows,
And I just try to die.

And I'm buried in the sand,
With caffeine on my lips, and water in my hands.
I try, but then I pour it out,
I couldn't take a drink,
Because I'm drowning in drought.

My lips so chapped,
I couldn't kiss my love.
Even if he stayed,
So I just give up.
And if my tongue were dry,
Dryer than it is now.
I could say goodbye,
Leaving my baggage without.

It's my life,
It's how I want to live.
I may just wanna shout,
Or maybe I just may...

... drown in a drought...

38.

Ripped Apart

I sat outside wait for,
A cigarette;
A chance to self-sabotage,
A chance to forget,
All the things that you did,
Keep on running through my head,
A painted portrait,
Of the living dead.

And I know it's my fault,

I should have never gotten in with you.
And I closed the vault,
To my inner feelings too.

Find myself in bed,
With a stranger in the day.
I can't understand why there is no fore play.

I am scared,
I am teared,
I am ripped apart,
Cry all day.

After you did your thing to me,
You kicked me out of the house,
I walk home shaking and lost,
Wondering where I am now.

Freaking out, fundamentally wrong in the head.
You opened up my flower,
But now my flower is dead.

And I know it's my fault,
And I wish it were different.
On better circumstances,
This may have been where I went.

Lying on my back,
You push hard,
I close my eyes.
I don't want to visualize all your dirty little lies.

"Be prepared",

Said I, scared,
I am ripped apart,
My world dies.

And the harder you make things,
By shutting off my switch,
The harder you thrust and I hide my screams,
My dreams, I see it.

You don't care,
Stole my bear,
All my teddy dreams,
In my mind.

You say that I wanted it because I didn't say no,
Well I don't think, people think I did, but I really don't
know.
I am shattered,
Beaten, battered,
I'm lying here,
Watching you go down,
Down,
Down...
On me...

Stepping stones turn to water,
I can see it.
I can taste all the mulberries,
I've had as a kid.
I can remember me playing on the playground with
my friends,
I remember it all, but this is where my childhood
ends...

And I couldn't say no..,
It's easy...
But you, I just didn't know,
You threw away my key.
Was there a gun?
Why did I run?
I thought it was innocence,
Thought chill meant fun...

I won't open my legs now,
They're closed for season,
You opened them yourself without giving a reason.

My heart yells,
But in hell,
You just shut your mouth,
Guilty to please...
I am scared,
I am teared,
I am ripped apart.

"Be prepared",
Said I, scared,
I am ripped apart,

Hard to bear,
But I swear,
I am ripped apart,
It's my fault.

39.

Cathouse

There's a brothel in between,
Addison drive and Rhenald street.
A courtesan happens to reside there,
And the men that touched a thigh wouldn't dare.

The house filled with a series of cobwebs,
And some lines of amphetamines.
Feels of a presence like maybe someone died,
And there's guilty sin inside...

In the bed that you lie.
Oh, the beautiful,
Treasures that lie within,
Cathouse.
Oh, the beautiful,
Treasures that lie within,
Cathouse.

He walks into Cathouse and catches her dancing,

He wears his light brown beret, she wears her laced-
up lingerie.

He pays her to lap dance, he touches her bosom,
She slaps him a new one and she plays the victim.
Cathouse mother comes in, she's really infuriated,
She makes him pay extra during,
The sin.

And he can't quite keep up with her,
And,
He can't pay for the good time either.
She ties him up and leaves him for dead,
In a body bag,
Back in the trash can.
Then back to bed she lies.

She lies in...

Filth, dirt,
Self sabotage hurt,
And the bedsheets are stained,
With emotional pain.
Let go of worries,
She says to herself,
That she has no time for selfish help.

She is...

A broke whore,
There's no more,
To say but,
She has scars on her arm,

From all of her cuts.
So she lies back as he has his own way,
Silent as a mouse,
In the Cathouse.

A broke whore,
There's no more,
To say but,
She has scars on her arm,
From of her cuts.
Lies back as he has his own way,
Silent as a mouse,
In the Cathouse.

Scenic

Strangled by static silence,
Leaving me here.
There's so much more that you must know, my dear.
Leaving me out in the frozen lake,
Just to freeze to death.

'Cause I have needed you here,
I have needed you near,
For so long I'm dying as spoken.
My heart shatters like glass,
This pain is everlast.
My mind,
Is insatiably frozen.

Oh and you just stand there,
I repair,
My moments,
You don't care.
Oh, the nightmare.

You need to sing to me,
Sing me to sleep,
Your soft voice,
Will heal me.
Oh, just trust me.

Your name it rings the bells,
Chiming in my head.
But yet you tell me to go to hell instead.

Your face it saves lullabies,
From beasts in the dark,
I can see them.
Oh, I can see them.

Mental health wanders,
Through pastures of mine.
Demonic ghosts just taking their sweet time.
I wait for them to eat away,
My thoughts and my life.
Is why I need you.
Oh, yeah, I need you.

Tape around my mouth,
Hiding self doubt,
Without you,
There's no way out.
Need the right route.

Now as I'm falling down,
You catch me now,
Easy is it,
You see how.
Oh, you need me now.

41.

Gen Z Rats

Beware, beware,
Of Gen Z rats.
The clothes they wear,
Could fit on Bratz.
They think they rule this world,
But a liberal bitch isn't,
Until they are winning.

So cry, cry, cry, cry,
Cry your little tears.
Cry them in your panties,
Because republicans cheered.
You don't want us to be complete,

You want to start a war,
Well that's just fine with me,
Because...

Gen Z doesn't play it easy,
Doesn't really play the games at all.
They're cheating,
Their looks are depleting,
Every time they're feeding to the snake holes.

One day you will see,
You will see, you will see,
Our world will crash down 'cause of Gen Z.

We chose, we chose,
Our president.
Then Gen Z went and ruined it.
They don't really know what they are voting for,
But it's popularity that they want, those attention
whores.

Lie, lie, lie, lie,
In that bed you made.
Because our hope will die,
Our whole country is at stake.
Look what you did, you've fucked it all up,
But you won't get away with it, you won't take the
golden cup.
Because...

Maybe one day,
You will stop your shit and say,
That it's too much,

But you've done it anyway.

And you can't take back,
What you did,
You seem to lack,
A functional brain, functional brain.

Help me understand,
Why the hell you're hurting not only our country but
yourself,
You make up these stupid rules,
And because of you,
We live in hell...

Rear View Mirror

You showed up absent,
Then I walked the plank,
That you had paid to be set up.

Your torture burns me,
Misshaped and lonely,
And you just leave me here fed up.

You wanted me for,
Music box nightmares,
In all my daydreams, can't get up.

Hey,
Can't you see,
I am right here?
I'm standing in view with my teddy bear.
Hey,
Can't you see,
I am right here?
I was all yours now it's unclear.
Look in your rear view mirror.

Angel, she told me,
That I'll be okay,
I've got a new soldier now.

He will take your place,
Not such a disgrace,
My voices, they are soft, not loud.

Music man, hold me,
Come back and see me,
You said you would, I don't see how.

Hey,
Can't you see,
I am right here?
I'm standing in view with your fifth beer.
Hey,
Can't you see,
I am right here?
Probably not, your visions unclear.
Look in your rear view mirror.

You say I am not yours,
You say I'm a liar,
You keep throwing wood into my fire.

Discharged from the psych ward,
It was my very first time,
Then you said it was my fault, I did the crime.

Why do you hate me,
Why do you disown me?
Why do you...
Why do you...
Why do you...
... leave...?
Hey,

Can't you see,
I am right here?

I'm standing in view with my soft tears.

Hey,
Can't you see,
I am right here?

I was all yours, now it's unclear.
Look in your rear view mirror..
Look in your rear view mirror...
Look in your rear view mirror...
Go have another beer...

43.

Bye Bye, Brain.

Find myself catching my daydreams,
Deep thoughts rip apart at the seams.
Inside all you'll find is my screams,
Wanting to get out so bad it sounds easy.

Why,
Can't I just die?

'Cause my brain is fried,

Somebody, you have to help me,
I'm getting worn like a trinket on a shelf.
Dusty, unused and waiting,
Just to be done, oh, just get me out of my brain.
Why,
Can't I just die?

My heart's breaking,
Hands are shaking.
And my motor,
It is raking.

I am brain dead,
I am brain dead,
I am brain dead.
Oh I am,
I'm just so brain dead...

Crazy Poem

Hey there, captured all your smiles in my mind.
Snowflakes fractured me in winter, thought I was
blind.
But then I see your eyes, they kind of look like mine.
Yours more of a darker tint align.
Champagne teardrops, better run and hide.

I was breathing too fast,
Heart was racing, body pacing,
Wanting you fast.
But I knew it was wrong,
I have let myself know all along,
That you'll never be more than a crazy song.

February was kind of scary, alone.
Valentine's Day came and went, I had no one.
I'd take you to my last years but I can't recall,
I am not okay, no, not at all.
But I see your picture, then I feel at home.

Kept my butterflies in jars,
And my daydreams back on Mars.
Played the field and played it hard,
Was the mechanic to my to cars.

Had a roaring bear to cross,
Had a lot that I have lost.
Oh, but I just count the cost,
Of all of the men I've put my paws on.

But when my car crashed,
I started new.
Thought I couldn't get back,
Then I noticed you.
It wasn't all like that,
I floated through...

Who knew...

I was breathing too fast,
Wanting a love so demented,
Finding it at last.
And I the tide I raced among,
Swam against the current, you float like a swan,
Both of us become,
A crazy poem.

44.

Mirror Dance

I look into you,
Remember the days,
I committed my sin.

My body, it haunts me,
How I could I ever,
Let that happen again.

I've left myself go,
So many times.
Leading me back here with my,
Out of control rhymes.

Take me away to,
A place of endearment.
A place where I'm not so...
Just let my have control.

I perform my mirror dance,
And here I go again.
Relapse road,
As I stand,
And watch me let go.
Watch me let go...

I find brilliance in adrenaline,
The high of branches,
The way of performing your sin.

And self control is beautiful,
You've got to get down that path.
And perform you mirror dance,
In perfection, poise, and wrath.

I don't need rehabilitation,
Not this time, I,
Need to set my station,
My empathy on high.

I can't stop once I start,
It stays with me.
My own beating heart,
Will again skip a beat.

But I don't care,
Death is hard to bear.
But my feelings are rare,
So with the world I will share.

I perform my mirror dance,
And here I go again.
Relapse road,
As I stand,
And watch me let go.
Watch me let go...

I look into you,
Remember the days,
I committed my sin.

45.

Damnation!

I cannot stand the way your eyes are watching,
They stare me down and I think I'm melting.
What a cynical surrounding,
Oh, how astounding.
How love could send me up in flames,
But very well drown me.

Cut so deep,
My heart you'll keep.
Oh, baby, just please do anything to send me to sleep.

I love you so I'll see you in hell,
The way you have me under your spell.
The shit you do, you do so well,
Just touch me, trust me, I'll never tell.

I will take your hand in filthy matrimony,
You can be my baby, I can be your honey.
I spill the bloodbath, you will come running,
Everything you say just makes me wanna die.

Love me deep, I want to enjoy the bleed,
Like broken paper hearts, we'll enjoy the screams.
People stare at us like we're the creeps,
But it's a starving life, we beg, we plead.

I now pronounce you sadist and sadene,
You will haunt the halls of this hellish scene.
You'll live forever in a bad dream,
And rule the castle of the damned as king and queen.

46,

SchizoFREEme

Schizophrenia I am,
I have nowhere to stand.
I'll never perfect God's plan,
According to you and your man.
You take your problems out on me,
And you won't even believe,
The hate that I received,

And the problems that lie at my feet.

Food is a problem,
Spending money is a problem,
In reality, I try to solve them.
Childhood mentality,
You say I have it in me,
I'll never be something great, because you see.

Caved in caverns, I stand tall,
I just want to say fuck it all.
My shallow breath I try to hide,
But my strongest suit starts to die.
Your pillow talk,
Your stolen crown.
I won it all,
Yet you take me down.

The proof is written in the sky,
Up so high,
That for you I'd die,
I'll never trust anyone again,
It's the end,
I can't pretend,
To be okay anymore.

47.

Guilt

On the day you passed,
My emotions were ever-last,
Why did you fall out of this world?
I had said some shit,
I just couldn't put up with it,
Our family is not quite the pearl.

But because of me,
We weren't invited to your wakening,
That guilt still holds right on to me.
How dare I make this,
All about my cold-hearted self?
There's no excuse except I need help.

I harbor guilt;
I harbor shame,
I harbor slander on my first name.
I've sewn the quilt,
To a dysfunctional dame,
How dare you say we're all the same!
We're not the same!
We're not the same!
How dare you say we're all the same!

Inside my head,
Over and I am shooting dead,
The girl that haunts inside my brain.
Alter ego, she,
Tries to fight and get the best of me,
I know you're bathing in pain.

But don't you worry,

You're up in Heaven now.
You're having the time of your life.
Borrowed your heart from you,
It was shiny and new.
Then I had to stab that shot with my knife.

Uncle Craig,
I miss you so,
I cry and ask where did you go?
It's not safe,
The route you take.
Oh, for heaven's sake,
Be afraid of my fate.

48.

Untitled

Self destruction,
Is my perfection.
If only you knew my dark side,
You'd want to run and hide.
Running away from every problem,
While everyone else tries to solve them.
Bitches will be bitches,
So let them be bitches.
But if they break your heart,
Rip them to shreds.

(I don't know I kind of just want to go away right
now.)

49.

Goodbye.

My mother told me to worry about my health,
I kind of scare her when I mutilate myself.

That January,
Was pretty scary.
I'm not going to lie,
I didn't really want to die.
But sixteen is too young to be worrying about death,
And I couldn't help it but the waters I did test.
Now I'm 29,
I still am not fine.
'Cause I didn't know that he'd change his mind,
About me.
It's been many years but now I see,
I came forth to God and on my knees,
I prayed to him, begging him please.

Take this pain away from my heart,
Give me the strength to make a new start.
His name carved in my mind then we part.
I think about all of the times for you, I starved.

Early December, he stayed in my room,
We made out in my bed all afternoon.
He respected my boundaries and I thank him for that.
But then February, alone I just sat.
And now I've lost my own mind as if it existed before,
You took all that's left of me the slammed the door.
You know I am ill, you know I can't take,
All that you've thrown away, the mess you have
made.
But now I'll just,
Remember the love and not the lust,
I'll remember how you lost my trust,
And maybe I won't feel in love anymore.
But I'll miss you forevermore.

50.

My Best Friend, Schizophrenia.

All the wasted tears,
All my deepest fears,
Happened with you.

My life was okay,
But I woke up today,
With the blues.

And I promised to myself,
That I would get help,
Before.

But now that's it late,
Don't think I can wait,
Anymore.

You have me so screwed,

Blued,
And tattooed.

I can't even think,
I'm on the brink,
Of being ever doomed.

And I could tell you that I miss,
My old life, not this,
But it'd be a lie.

'Cause even though you're rude,
And very crude,
You have become my life.

Life is miserable,
But that's so resistible,
Because you're here.

Schizophrenic girl,
But she has her whole world,
Ahead of her.

You may be a demon,
But I'm feening,
You.

Why? Because I can,
No else understands,
My truth.

So please don't go away,
Please stay.

You are my best friend.

You are here for life,
Until the knife,
Gives us both an end.

And I was kind of afraid,
My bed wasn't made,
For you yet.

But I love you, please don't leave,
I don't want to have to grieve,
My best friend.

Sleepless In Destin

I'd take it back,
I'd give my heart and soul.
Just for your return,
I'm in this world so cold.

And I knew right then,
That you'd walk in that store,
Then who's to say,
That I won't believe anymore?

Because I would never let you die,
I'd keep you safe, I'd hug you tight.
They messed up, those cops they had no right,
Now I'm sleepless in Destin, I'm wishing you a
pleasant night.

If I saw their face,
Those cops, I tase them back.
I'd get them good,
Make them have a heart attack.

I'm so hurt by them,
They've taken everything.
They've taken my whole world,
They've taken my uncle Craig.

Those assholes,
The cops they took my life.
Now I'm sleepless in Destin,

I'm wishing you a pleasant night.

52.

Lucky

Ambulance came;
Sending me right back,
Asthma attack.

I woke up fine;
In the ICU,
To astound you.

Doctor said that I'm one of those patients,
In which whom are lucky.
And that's all thanks to my Lord and Savior,
The road was so rocky.

2 months premie;
Born two months early,
Into the world.

I came out suffering;
But I survived,
I am alive.

I believe;
God, Jesus,
Eternity.

Mother picked up and held me,
In her heart, love was wealthy.
Mother kissed my forehead,
Glad that I was not dead.
Life is so beautiful, so grand.
Worth it in the end.
Worth it in the end.

53.

Living On Ground

They take me miles,
To tropical wastelands;
I love my fans.

They read my books;
They love my stories;
All my glory.

They think I have a pretty good lifeline,
A pretty good author.
Or at least that's what I'd like to believe,
'Cause it's all I have to offer.

I don't have much,

For this country;
I feel dumpy.

I pretend I'm a bestseller,
Though I make zilch,
I live on psych pills.

Nobody will understand me,
I think that it's okay.
But with all of my self-harming issues,
It's hard letting me stay.

You gotta believe in yourself...

They think that it is so easy,
Being an author is easy.
They think that writing is easy,
They think writing is easy.

It's not as easy as it sounds...
Living on ground...
Living on ground...
Living on ground...

54.

Love Makes No Mistakes

You're here at my doorstep, knocking on the door,
The look upon your face makes evil look pure.

You lean in to kiss me, flowers in your hand,
A second without you is one I can't stand.

Why,
Would I ever lie?
I can't imagine life without this guy.
I know,
Someday he'll go,
They always leave, always leave me, oh no.

Go,
Fetch my things,
I'll meet you at your place,
Give your doorbell a ring.
The chance I will take,
Because love makes no mistakes.

The love in the blankets, romance in the sheets,
Being with you, my heart is complete.
This isn't cliché, this isn't a lie,
My love for you will never ever die.
Wait, I can't make of this meaning,
Have I been dreaming?
Why do they all say watch out?
Is it him I should be worried about?

Go,
Fetch my things,
I'll meet you at your place,
Give your doorbell a ring.
The chance I will take,
Because love makes no mistakes.

What do they know?
It'll be over and then we can go.
Pack up your ammo,
Because they've gots guns and they always kill slow.

Go,
Fetch my things,
I'll meet you at your place,
Give your doorbell a ring.
The chance I will take,
Because love makes no mistakes.

55.

I Hope You Know

When I saw your face through my screen,
I knew then and there,
Then and there,
That you were the one for me.

And since then, I've dreamt of your face,
Magic in the air,
In the air,
That I am in a safer place.
I think I'm going to stay right here,
I hope you don't disappear.

'Cause your face, porcelain, painted well,

You've got me under your spell.
Oh.
Your eyes are so enticing,
I just hope you know,
That I get sad every now and then,
But you like me the way I am,
Oh.
Your smile is mesmerizing,
I just hope you know.

You know I'm ill, mentally, kind of insane,
Oh, but you like me,
You like me,
You like me anyway.

I've only known you for a little time,
But I'm already hooked,
I am hooked,
Overdrive, you are my new high.
I hope I don't scare you off, but well,
I just cannot help myself.

'Cause your face, porcelain, painted well,
You've got me under your spell.
Oh.
Your eyes are so enticing,
I just hope you know,
That I get sad every now and then,
But you like me the way I am,
Oh.
Your smile is mesmerizing,
I just hope you know.

I just want to touch,
You and your sweet essence oh so much.
And someday I will see,
That face in person I've been missing dearly.

Wanna get to know you better,
We'd be trendsetters,
We'd be trendsetters.
Wanna get to know you better,
We'd be trendsetters,
We'd be trendsetters.

'Cause your face, porcelain, painted well,
You've got me under your spell.
Oh.
Your eyes are so enticing,
I just hope you know,
That I get sad every now and then,
But you like me the way I am,
Oh.
Your smile is mesmerizing,
I just hope you know.

Sad Truth

I'm no musician,
But my heart can listen to the words.
Oh, it hurts.
My lungs try singing,
Bagpipes ringing like a phone.
No one's home.
I see the rail, I lean against it.
Fall off in no time, defenseless.

The sad truth,
Is my soul is not whole,
And I'd like to be a perfect being.
And who knew,
Music is my soul,
Behold,
It's what I'm living.
I'm sad I can't sing,
Sad I can't breathe.
But I'm going to keep on giving.

Lead me to stardom,
But not fame, just reality,
Oh, me.
Can't quite figure out,
Who I should truly be.
But it's okay,
Life is more real this way.
I've made up my mind,

Just to leave to be

I'm so stuck on your negativity,
Why can't you just be like me?
Then I look back and think,
There's more to life than to find that missing link.

57.

I'll See You Soon

The massacre,
Occurred,
When I laid eyes on her.
I knew I had,
To have you.
We resonate,
It's fate.
Be warned,
Your heart,
I might break.

I'll see you soon.
I'll see you soon.
An honest mistake, babe,
You could mistake the hearts I break,
For someone saved.
Oh, God, oh my,
I think I've died,
In your arms tonight.

58.

Move Along

Looking back at all the fun times we had,
I'd tell you,
No need to be sad, you're the best that I've had,
We both lose.
My dark versioned Kari,
You are very scary,
But you're so right.

I glance at the mirror, all I see is fear,
Don't you know.
What happened to you, because now all you do,
Is go slow.
Hurting yourself,
Knowing you don't need help,
You have no control.
Well this song is in fact,
About the way you act,
Your mind's dull.

Dear old self,
Come back and stay on the shelf.
No rainy days.
You have been gone for too long,
Now all we have is a song,
About how you're gone.

Dear myself,
You can just go straight to hell.
Drop dead, you said,
That my one version's true,
I don't want that to be you,
I can't move on.

Move along.

Well I have a knack for fighting a war,
With my own head.
But my thorns have come up so easily,
Injuring me,
Roses dead.
And it's okay now, I have lied in the ground,
For too long, it's time,
For my light to shine,
Time to take back what's mine,
Spare a dime.

You have a great way of saying,
This game you're not playing.
You always blame other people,
For shame.

Oh Miss Kari,
Where did she,
Run off, she's missing.
It's for her own good,
She's gone now, knock on wood.

But she left her mind,
It will kill you with time,
She'll never return.
You've got your own matches,
Gasoline wreaked havoc,
Burn, baby, burn...

Move along...
Move along...

I just cannot move on…
Move along.

59,

Crying With Diffraction Glasses

Crying on my doorstep,
I open up the door.
Shaking from the downpour,
Collapses to the floor.

I ask,
"Did he do it again?
Did he hurt you even more?"
She shrugged her shoulders.

Her champagne smile,
Has turned into Miller frown.
I want to know what's going on with her,
And why she's so down.

So I ask her again,
Why she never comes around,
Her voice grew colder.
She said…

I haven't been myself lately,
Greatly,
Appreciated that you see.
'Cause I don't don't want to ever be,
Outspoken.

Cousin I think I know what's going on,
And,
My whole life is falling apart.
I just want to go back to start,
I'm broken.

So we picked up the champagne glasses,
Toasted to a new life.
"To hell with that asshole,
To hell with being his wife."

She said,
"I think I'll resurrect.
Think I'll come back from the dead.
Im getting older."

I haven't been myself lately,
Greatly,
Appreciated that you see.
'Cause I don't don't want to ever be,
Outspoken.

Cousin I think I know what's going on,
And,
My whole life is falling apart.
I just want to go back to start,
I'm broken.

She just filed for divorce,
Took him to court,
Filed papers and everything.

And then he was long gone,
The restraining order strong,
Now she can finally sing...

I haven't been myself lately,
Greatly,
Appreciated that you see.
'Cause I don't don't want to ever be,
Outspoken.

Cousin I think I know what's going on,
And,
My whole life is falling apart.
I just want to go back to start,
I'm broken.

Can You Feel The Love Tonight?

Dark night, Omni,
His hand, my knee.
I feel at peace,
He's got the suite.

We call a cab ride,
The city tonight,
Looks just right,
The buildings, the light.

You can see in the streetlights,
You hear it as the car drives.
You can smell the perfume just right,
Can you feel the love tonight?
Can you feel the love tonight?

61.

Firearms

She awakens just in time,
Her skin silky smooth,
Her lips like wine.
And I roll her right over,
And kiss her tight,
In the middle of the night.

My cellphone goes off by the bed,
Clock strikes one and the lights are red,
She groans up against me, down she heads,
And that's it, I'm already dead...

Her body's firearms,
And I am going,
Down, down, down.

This is it, all over me.
She's going,

Down, down, down.

And the wars are silenced now.

She hops in my convertible whip,
I take her home, I bite her lip.
Tell her "goodbye, I'll see you,
Tomorrow night,
Before the sun shines.

And that's when grabbed my face,
Sucked me motionless,
And I wouldn't want to waste,
The adorable kiss.

So I took her inside her house,
Silent as a mouse,
Dragged her by her feet,
Threw her on the bed and I was complete.

Her body's firearms,
And I am going,
Down, down, down.

This is it, all over me.
She's going,
Down, down, down.

And the wars are silenced now.

Pulling her blonde hair,
What's under there, what's under there?
Tie her to a living chair,

Deep in despair, deep in despair.

Her body's firearms,
And I am going,
Down, down, down.

This is it, all over me.
She's going,
Down, down, down.

And the wars are silenced now.

Starry Eyes

I saw the truth, I saw it all,
My name cursed on a bathroom stall.
The man I married is no man to me,
After our wedding night you made me see.

You called me names during sex,
Shortly after you became my ex.
I said I loved you, you thought it was real,
Now come on, tell me, how the fuck do you feel?

Was it all a waste of time trying to make you see,
That all that should've have been on your mind was
me?

Blind eyes never see through the glass,
Wise eyes always see through the past.
Kind eyes took your love at hand,
But your starry eyes have failed me again.
Again, again.

Come on do it, blame me again,
We never even started off friends.
That was the first mistake I made,
Red flags at Six Flags, couldn't concentrate.

Your key was devotion,
But when it came to motion,
You had to spill your potion,
Now have fun with your lotion...

I needed a cigarette,
After the rough sex,
It wasn't fun but it set,
Me free.

I couldn't believe your words,
And it still makes me hurt,
I always did put you first,
You better believe.

If you would have shown,
Your one shot you had in life,
You would've had not known,
And you would've put down the knife...

Blind eyes,
Never see through the glass...
Wise eyes,
Always see through the past...
Kind eyes
Took your love at hand...
Your starry eyes...
They've failed me...

63.

Scar Sister

Twenty-nine,
Says she's doing fine,
But she's got a secret.

Wants to die,
Hurts herself at night,
Found out its defects.

She just wants somebody to love,
Somebody to care.
But she refuses to tell a soul,
So no one's aware.

She's just a girl, a lonely soul,
Trapped inside a woman.
Three years ago,
Her happiness,
Never returned again.

She just needs some therapy,
She just some fine festivities,
Wants to be free.
But nothing works, under her shirt,
That razor blade just doesn't work.
If only she could leave…

More pressure,
On her when that skirt,
Didn't fit her.
She sticks,
Two fingers down her throat,
To make herself purge.

She says she's sober now,
But looks can really deceive.
They think there's nothing wrong,
They think she's overcome her disease.

The girl decides to open up,
About her problems.
Her friends near and far away,
Help her solve them.

She's grateful for the while,
She spent talking to them.

She tries to bring a smile,
To her face, she still wants to leave.

Rock Bottom

Take the razor blade out of my hand,
I've relapsed, I'm afraid that it'll never get easier
now.
I can't take all the guilt anymore,
I can't buy what you sell, and I'm off of the market, I
vow.

So I pour my heart out here,
And I write my sorrows down,
Someday I'll be yours,
The crown,
Someday you won't be bored.
One day I will be what you want.

Starve myself so I'm thin, it don't work,
I just wanna dive in, but these people 'round here are
all jerks.
When I want to escape, I set sail,
And nobody believes that this life I have never will
prevail.

I am so untalented,
I'm ugly and unbalanced.
I just want this to end,
I wish I was trying to pretend...
And I'm so sorry...
You can blame all your problems on me...

65.

Marching Band Of Evil Spirits

The words come in mind,
They are pouring like rain.
Leaving wounds and blisters,
Getting deeper with pain.
Fracturing my skull,
It's too dull to find answers.

I get questions asked,
Normalcy days,
Like what's wrong with you?
Or are you okay?
I stay quiet yet polite,
Though this shit eats me like cancer.

I march to the marching band of evil spirits.
I live with them.

They're inside me I can't hide,
I'd show my pride,
But if I might do so,
The demons will glide.
They'll eat me alive,
'Til I break down and cry black poison.

These are my voices,
I know they're not real.
But they're here and it feels,
Like they're steering my wheel.
I can feel, I can touch,
I am such in a rush,
Because they never leave me alone.
I just wanna go home.

Demons told me,
That what I see,
Is within me.
It's within.

Wicked smiles and,
Now they're your friends.
Until the end,
Never ends...

Phone Her, Stoner.

I,
Have held onto the innocence of our first
conversation.
Why,
I still don't know but get this, it just don't fit the
situation.

'Cause now,
You've moved on ever so slightly to the next chair
over there.
And now,
She looks at me as a stranger, dangling her hands in
her hair.

She's beauty, she's grace…
Now she's all over your face…

Tell me,
Is it wrong,
To write a song about how you left?

Is it safe to admit,
That I feel like shit?
The girl committed theft.

And I'll be,
I knew all along,
Where we went wrong,
Was the table you set.

Your person,
She's worse than myself,
You I can't help my tongue just yet.

When,
You look into her eyes,
Do you see that hope,
That you need?

Because I,
Feel that we with me,
You'd get the freedom,
You just have to wait and see.

And your heart seems to whine,
When it intertwines,
With somebody else.

And our love will never fail,
It will prevail,
I know well.

She's pumpkin, she's pie…
Now she's smeared all over your eyes…

Tell me,
Is it wrong,
To write a song about how you left?

Is it safe to admit,
That I feel like shit?
The girl committed theft.

And I'll be,
I knew all along,
Where we went wrong,
Was the table you set.

Your person,
She's worse than myself,
You I can't help my tongue just yet.

I know you smoke pot,
I know you have no job,
I know you aren't good for me,
But your heart I tried to rob.

I finally went bankrupt when I found you,
When I found out you found her,
We had something going.
Guess I lost sight of where you were.

Tell me,
Is it wrong,
To write a song about how you left?

Is it safe to admit,
That I feel like shit?
The girl committed theft.

And I'll be,
I knew all along,
Where we went wrong,
Was the table you set.

Your person,

She's worse than myself,
You I can't help my tongue just yet.

Goodbye...
Goodbye...
Goodbye...
Goodbye...
Goodbye...

67.

For Better Or For Worse

Just pick up the bottle,
Scream until your heart stops,
Wait until the dewdrops,
Drip down from the rain.

Nobody knows you,
Why are you still alive,
Maybe you should just die,
To get rid of your suffer and pain.

'Cause I am here to tell you,
You're better off dead.
I'm one of the voices,
Living in your head.

You find me confusing,
Say you were here first.
I think it's amusing,
I am here for better or for worse…

And when they come to save you,
I'll stop each and every one,
I'll even give you the gun,
Aren't I your best friend?

I'm a good person,
You just need to realize,
They're feeding you with lies,
This is how it's gonna end.

'Cause I am here to tell you,
You're better off dead.
I'm one of the voices,

Living in your head.

You find me confusing,
Say you were here first.
I think it's amusing,
I am here for better or for worse...

I've come again to haunt you,
Slit your fucking wrists,
Nobody even cares that you exist.

I'm your precious angel,
Godparent at best,
I'll be here 'til I force you to lay yourself at rest.

'Cause I am here to tell you,
You're better off dead.
I'm one of the voices,
Living in your head.

You find me confusing,
Say you were here first.
I think it's amusing,
I am here for better or for worse.

68.

Delicious

I'm walking down Magic Hall,
In my old high school, then I see you.
Tells me I won't kiss a girl,
Though I told him I love to.

But he didn't believe me, no,
So I went on straight up to you…

Her kiss delicious, yeah.
I'm getting off now, ooh.
Tell me all I want to hear,
I keep on staring at you.
And I love everything you do.

I'm safe in Heaven now,
I've got everything I need.
We have our next go round,
I develop my fantasy.

No, why are you leaving now?
I want you by my side…
We split our paths and we,
We had made our history.
Though we never saw each other again.

We have let it go to waste,
But if I see that pretty face,
I'd have to reside myself in sin…

69.

Kiss The Stars

I met you
Out in the courtyard,
The other day.
Mama stood,
Like a prison guard,
Said go away.

Then last night,
I heard a noise outside my window.
Open the pane,
And you call my name.

So be,
Patient,
Patient,
At night,
Just kiss the stars.

So be,
Patient,
Patient,
At night,
Just kiss the stars.

I saw you,
In the mall buying clothes.
We snuck away,
Went in the changing room,
You know how that goes.

Came back home,
You tossed rocks again,
I told you to go.
Though I loved you so,
I loved you so.

So I guess,
This is how it's gonna end.
Just remember our first kiss,
No, we can't pretend.

I sit out,
In the courtyard,
Staring at the moon,
Remembering the day,
You took me and I swooned.
So be patient.

70

Hydrated

They tell me to leave,
I have no intention to do what you've mentioned of
me.
Now I have the key,
I know how to hurt you, now I can desert every
being.

Before all of this,
I had a bad nightmare the night where you said I was
gone.
But you're full of shit,
I can't go, I won't go, I guess you were wrong all
along.

The bitterness contains me…
It's eating up my soul…
My body is detaining…
I'm feeling so unholy…

"Now drink up all your last words" kids are telling
me,
There's no reason you should be yelling.
Say you love, you've got to be kidding me,

Who's hydrated now?

Thirsty, I am,
But I will plead to you that I am a dangerous girl.
I've seemed to leave land,
But mine is still drought and I will not go pout to the
damned.

Yes, dehydration,
Will not drown your sea of control.
You are the castle,
Your moats are just parched up dirt holes.

71.

The Devil Wears Prada

Oh my, oh my, just watch your back,
The sky, the sky's under attack,
This guy he lies right back,
Watching all of the others who destroy their lovers.

Cry, cry, baby, take your lollipop,
You know that one that makes all of the panties drop.

Climb on inside of the dirty paws,
Of a single slut bag, releasing her claws on you.

So careful...

Ladies, they all seem to love you,
They all seem to rub it in my face.
Ladies, please just step aside,
I see through his lies,
I cannot take it.
So when I get home tonight,
We will fight, we will fight,
And I will smash his fucking face in.

Just go, just go, you've done enough,
Although you're here acting so tough.
I cannot deal with all the hazardous hoes here,
I cannot deal with my pillow full of dry tears.

Bad boy, bad boy, you are not my type,
I would rather marry someone I would die for.
I'll save my gun for somebody else;
Someone more important, you can just go die in a
cell.

So careful...

Ladies, they all seem to love you,
They all seem to rub it in my face.
Ladies, please just step aside,
I see through his lies,
I cannot take it.
So when I get home tonight,

We will fight, we will fight,
And I will smash his fucking face in.

The day will arrive,
When you all get a bad disease,
And I will laugh as I am herpes free.
Maybe it's done,
Maybe you have truly changed.
And we will live again so happily.

Where's my camera?
The look on your face, though,
I'd love to show you what you're missing,
I can't believe you thought that was real.
I am happy, you are sad,
Come on, don't you get mad.
Before I laugh,
Just say cheese!

Ladies, they all seem to love you,
They all seem to rub it in my face.
Ladies, please just step aside,
I see through his lies,
I cannot take it.
So when I get home tonight,
We will fight, we will fight,
And I will smash his fucking face in.

And I will smash his fucking face in,
And I will smash his fucking face in.

-inspired by Set It Off's 'Wolf In Sheep's Clothing'

Bad Timing...

The slits,
On your wrists,
Tell a story.
Never boring.

They say,
That death's okay,
But just remember,
Your heart is ember.

The truth,
Is that you,
Would rather lie down,
Than have a showdown.

Embrace,
Your silly ways,
Of self infliction.
You're the victim.

Well, you haven't said it yet,
But I know this hurts your head,

The things that people say,
They just get in the way.

And your health may be at risk,
But you want to throw your fists,
At the people, get in line,
You are wasting your own time.

The shells,
Off the shelf,
Are only witnessed,
To blame your fitness.

Your death,
Catch your breath,
Just live in spite of,
Those nasty spiders.

Tell me again,
Why should they win…

Well, you haven't said it yet,
But I know this hurts your head,
The things that people say,
They just get in the way.

And your health may be at risk,
But you want to throw your fists,
At the people, get in line,
You are wasting your own time.

I know you want to die
(Know you want to die),

I know you want to cry
(Know you want to cry).
Put the razor blade down
(Razor blade down),
Come and grab your own crown
(Grab your own crown).

You are wasting your own time…

Well, you haven't said it yet,
But I know this hurts your head,
The things that people say,
They just get in the way.

And your health may be at risk,
But you want to throw your fists,
At the people, get in line,
You are wasting your own time.

And you haven't said it yet,
But those voices in your head,
Are just a silly, troubled way,
That you yourself portray.

And your health may be at risk,
But you want to throw your fists,
At the people, get in line,
You are wasting your own time.

At the people, just stop trying,
You are wasting your own time.

Lies And Lullabies

I need more time,
To read between your lines,
And your disguise.
Tell me again,
The reason why you lied,
You hid your pride.

I see right through,
The games you play.
You threw away today.

I can't believe,
You did this to me.
Call me a fool,
For loving you.

I've been deceived,
But it's not the first time,
You threw away,
My secrets, lies and lullabies.

I talked to mom,
About the things you said and did to me.
She said we'll talk,
About it later when she is free.

It's just so hard,

The deck of cards that I've been dealt.
But you chose to fall,
And drag me with you on your way to hell.

Asphyxiate me,
Do it again and again.
Fingers like knives into my throat,
And choke me with your hands.

74.

Sleepless In Dallas

I let go,
You catch me from beneath.
The hands I hold,
Are just pure deceit.

And the air is cold,
Your skin was so soft.
I could just run,
But I think I'll just sleep it off.

Right now,
I'm looking overhead.
There's nothing but the crossbones,
Everything is dead.

I vow,
To never take the stream.
'Cause I am here in Dallas,
I'm wishing you sweet dreams.

Falling through,
Glass that once attacked.
What we once had,
There's no looking back.

I just want to know,
Why you had left me.
And I can't breathe,
I wonder if it ever gets easy.

I can't lie,
Life isn't what it seems.
'Cause I am here in Dallas,
I'm wishing you sweet dreams.

75

Dear Head

Long time no see, I had waited for you to come back,
Now that I've found you, I've fallen back off the
tracks.
Lost in translation,
Needing a vacation,
I can't hold back.
I'm wanting temptation,
To rid my Damnation,
It's what I lack.

My fear is you'll leave again but my hope is you'll
always return,
I'm getting too old, I can't fix the bridges I've burned.
Calling a cab,
For my ever blue sadness,
I'm so damn screwed.
Desolation has,
A way to just grab,
My neck wrung by noose.

Dear head,
I know that you just want me dead,
I won't give up yet.
I've tried playing nice,
But I give up the fight,

I won't think twice.

Dear head,
I don't mean those words that I said,
You've kept all my debts,
Now I'm headed to the pen,
Of mentality prison,
Don't think you'll see me again.
Goodbye, friend.

Well, I have a knack for finding the facts out of fiction,
And not to brag but I kind of can haggle my vision.
I don't see selective,
But I can reject,
What things I see.
It's crazy at best,
But that's just life I guess,
It's part of me.

This is an understanding,
Of what I've been handed.
No, Brain, you won't win, why can't I just fit in?
It won't be too long,
'Til I am too far gone.
I hadn't seen in years my final breath, last tears.
But I want to know why you've traded me in, I need
to know why,
You belong in my brain and I've gone insane, I'm rye.

76.

Ashes Fly

We started out like a family;
There were no more wars overseas.
We had it together like Switzerland,

We were a full circle, we had no end.

Then things got tough when she arrived;
She had those captivating eyes.
Showed me what it's like to live my life,
Then turned around and showed me how to die.

She was my whole world and so were they,
We made a spark.
Now I'm faded, I'm left in the dark.

My ashes fly,
Swarm around the blood red sky.
All the stars will slowly fade away and die.

I just need,
Someone to remember me.
Someone to have faith in me,
So I can finally sleep.

It's not okay that I feel this way,
Maybe I'm just blind and I'm okay.
But have you ever swam in your sorrows?
I can't be alone,
I can't stay.

Now listen up clearly,
It's happening yearly.
My thoughts I now feel,
No control of the wheel.

Pay close attention,
Like her, I won't mention.

My mind's in detention,
Recess intermission...

77.

She's Out There

Close my eyes so tightly,
Listening to voices in my head,
Am I alive or am I dead?
These words better unsaid.
Reality has eyes so red.
Mmm, under my bed...

...eyes so red...

Can't tell what is fake or is real,
I sense it all, can touch, can feel.
My horror, endless movie reel,
Just watch them closely, how they steal.

I've been gone but I'm back here again,
I'm here to represent this awful wretch.

(She tries to take my heat,
Her darkness I can't defeat.)

I went away, now I'm back here for more,
My suicide is based on a vengeful whore.
(Someone save me 'fore I go,
And pull something so low.)

Here I am lying in a cage,
Boxed up, I have given up rage.
I can't fight, 'cause I can't win,
So I back up, give up again.

Back in action, back to black,
Darkness forms and demons attack.
Voices carry, visions blur,
Oh, please don't take me back to her.

My beating heart is now a shattered stone,
You can leave me but please don't leave me alone.
I just want out of this life,
But I don't want to die.

You think I'm wrong but I know I'm right,
Before too long I'll be saying goodnight.
You don't know what I've been through,
You'll never know the abuse.

Here I am lying in a cage,
Boxed up, I have given up rage.
I can't fight, 'cause I can't win,
So I back up, give up again.

Back in action, back to black,
Darkness forms and demons attack.
Voices carry, visions blur,
Oh, please don't take me back to her.

Here I am lying in a cage,
Boxed up, I have given up rage.
I can't fight, 'cause I can't win,
So I back up, give up again.

Back in action, back to black,
Darkness forms and demons attack.
Voices carry, visions blur,
Oh, please don't take me back to her.

I roar like a lion,
Screaming but nobody hears a thing,
I'm off on my very own again.
I told you I can't win,
Don't believe when they say you're wrong,
Disbelieve,
In what you have showed,
Your reality.

78.

Pretty Eyes

Your tears of joy flooded my sea,

Your doubt of faith made me disbelieve.
I don't know why you have left me.
I'm in in an empty seat filled with empty dreams.

And most my songs are about you,
And I live the way I didn't used to.
I used to watch and gaze at your every move.
I'm a fool for having fallen for you.

Out of all the stars at night,
You seem to shine the brightest.
I know we didn't work out, but,
You're still my pretty eyes.

Lovely pants and that plaid green shirt,
Then you left me, now I'm hurt.
The way you touched my thighs,
You're still my pretty eyes.

We had a love like perfection,
We did some things I'll never mention.
You slept in my deprivation.
I look into the sky, it's where you reside.

You shine bright like lily lightly,
The only pony who means much to me.
But Applejack was your favorite,
She had that pony smile that you saw in me.

Out of all the stars at night,
You seem to shine the brightest.
I know we didn't work out, but,
You're still my pretty eyes.

Lovely pants and that plaid green shirt,
Then you left me, now I'm hurt.
The way you touched my thighs,
You're still my pretty eyes.

My pretty eyes...
My pretty eyes...
My pretty eyes...

Out of all the stars at night,
You seem to shine the brightest.
I know we didn't work out, but,
You're still my pretty eyes.

Lovely pants and that plaid green shirt,
Then you left me, now I'm hurt.
The way you touched my thighs,
You're still my pretty eyes.

That shirt I kept that night,
I held on to it tight.
I wore it every night,
For you, my pretty eyes.

I miss your fragile smile,
I miss your detailed dial.
Your tone, your body, I,
I miss your pretty eyes.

79.

Schizo Sadness

I started writing for a reason,
It was my only reason to live.
Got lost then found, the finder's keepers,
Then the finder lost me again.
Because they,

Broke my angel spirit,
Up to my ear I hear it,
It's coming close, endear it,
Schizo sadness.

My author life is over,
I'll never sell another,
I'm hiding under covers,

Schizo sadness.

They wanted my book, yes I know it,
But only because I'm ill.
So they decided just to throw it,
They bought it, but sad I am still.

Juicy couture and Diamonds,
I'll never try to find them,
My moment's wasted on my,
Schizo sadness.

My love was pure for writing,
Got lost in all my sightings,
Guess it was too exciting,
Schizo sadness.

My music failed and all my art,
Never thought I'd be a part,
Of all this madness mayhem,
My chest can't breathe, I'm falling down now.

Lucifer wrapped in a bow,
Never tells you to let go,
But in his mind he's saying, "no,
I want you down on flame row."

Hell is a clubhouse, earth is a tree,
Heaven is a tree trunk not made for me.
So I climb the highest, to get to the top,
Reside in the clubhouse and make frequent drops.

I wouldn't had such a lovely life,

But instead I am crazy as shit,
So I quit.
They looked up and they had lied,
So for the last time...

You broke my angel spirit,
I'm not around to hear it,
All of the things you've endeared,
My schizo sadness.

My author life is over,
I'll never write another,
Book just so I get smothered,
My schizo sadness...

I'll never write another,
Schizo sadness...

Obsessed.

My life is chaotic,
It's gone awry.
The train that's rolling on it's tracks,
Got derailed tonight.
I am howling at the moon,
While lying in my bed.
Knowing the morning will arrive soon,
But I cannot get out of my head.

I turn my tv off finally to get much needed sleep,
I'm sick of hungering for the chance to keep my
porcelain heart here on my sleeve.
It seems to have its way for justice,
Seems to have its way for greed.
It seems to have its way sickness,
Always has a way with me.

Awake and obsessed;
Taking off my tear-stained dress.
Letting them know that all my family was impressed.
Obsessed and consumed,
Tired of feeling doomed.
I want the world to know,
I'm not the monster you assumed.

I get it, guys, you're on the fence.
Believe me, I don't blame you.
I know I probably never make any sense,
But please tell me if I somewhat do.
It's sick way of wanting to live,
It's a sick way trying to give.
But with OCD tearing life out of me,
And schizophrenia along bipolar, you see,
I am not the woman you want me to be.
I am not the woman you're needing of me.

Awake and obsessed;
My hoping I'll pass this test,
The matter is I'm trying to give,
While trying to rid my mess.
Obsessed and consumed;
Living in this dark, evil room,
Wanting to get out,
I live I strive,
Just to die,
In a tomb.

And with a smile I wear that's attached to my heart,
Beating the shit out of myself, leaving me to starve.
But I play the victim, yeah, woe is me.
I am sorry about that, forgive me, I'm on my knees.
And if only I could make me go away,
I promise, this mess of mine,
Will clean in time,
And forever you'll stay,
Happy, I want it to be that way.

Awake and obsessed;

Please ignore me, I'm a major mess.
I have too many addictions in my bed,
They need to lay at rest.
Obsessed and consumed,
Mother, I just promise you,
That when you wake,
I'll be off the stake,
For you.

81.

Getaway Car

Hello;
I go by the name Karianne.
I know I'm not the best,
I've probably failed your test,
I am sorry.

I know;
It's imprinted in my mind.

It's me you cannot trust,
It's myself that I lust,
I always worry.

The money's in the bag;
Take it from my register.
Take the cash and run,
Take the cash and run,
Don't have to shoot me.

But if you want to jab;
Just do it, I surrender.
Just step up the counter,
Leave us encountered,
In a movie.

Rob;
Get back your getaway car.
Needing to sit still,
You just need your thrill,
Understand this.

I don't;
Want anything to do with this.
But maybe if I go,
You can run the show,
It's your business.

So judge all you want;
My favor is sunk right in you.
Do you even know,
That I'm letting you go,
And destroy me.

The internet it hurts,
But I'd let you hurt me even more.
You are such a tease,
You do what you please.
That's my story.

82.

Bottomless Pit

I have a breakdown,
Fall on my face.
I've reached my bottomless pit.

I watch as they play on,
The kids in the rain.
I'm not ready for this shit.

I was always the one who smiled,
The positive one, the bubbly one.
The one who took control of my odds.

I cut my golden hair,
I sing no more.
I can't remember when I last fought.

And these happy days,
Are nonexistent anymore.
And my selfish ways,
Are locking you out of my door.
Im locking you out.

My mind is full of,
Terrible things.
Monsters haunt me in the night,

Naïveté struck me as a child,
I'm still that child.
Nothing is going right.

I need somebody to,
Tell me I'm okay, to,
Let me know that I'm doing alright.

My nightmare glistens,
Keeps me awake.
The lovely tune, so light.

And these happy days,
Are nonexistent anymore.
And my selfish ways,
Are haunting me to the core.
To the core.

83.

Psycho In Disguise

The day has come to an end,
As the darkness sinks in,
If you search you may find,
Grandfather Thyme.

He's got many friends,
This is where it ends,
Grandfather sneaks in your room,
You shriek, you know you're doomed.

His friends all come in different shades,
Alexandra Axe and Paula Plague,
When Mother Murder comes out from your bed,
Oh, have you heard of her, she'll chop off your head.

Silent screams from Susie Scream,
Distant yells from Howie Hell.
Such a thrill for Kylie Kill,
Now you know these characters well.
Sexy slithers down your hallway,
Knock on your bedroom door, but wait—
There goes your eyes now,
GOUGE IT! GOUGE IT! GOUGE IT!

He's happy now that I've set him free,
Delicious as he looked, his heart now belongs to me...
Take the side rail, just hang on.
I've loved you once, never loved another.
Now I prey on your selfish, helpless mother.

Because she really means well,
Oh, but hold that thought.
I'm just an innocent man,
And I hope you bought,
That line,
Oh, my,
It's her time,
Goodbye.

And her freezing heart,
Is just a part,
Of her reflection of deception,
I hope you've learn your lesson.

I'm a psycho in disguise,
I gouged out your grey eyes.
You were so beautiful at least to me.
But shut your demise,
Your solitude lies.
You were so beautiful at least to me.
So listen from the wise.

Psychos, let's commence,
Let's jump that fence,
Into your neighbor's yard.
We'll make our entryways,
Into your dark Sunday's,
It's really not that hard.

I'd rather die, rather die,
Than live a lie, live a lie.
What was I thinking? What was I thinking?
My boat is sinking, boat is sinking.

I'll just say goodbye…

84.

There's No Use Crying Over Spilled INK

The story ends like this,
A simple cut to the wrist.
And once the wrist is slit,
You plead the fifth.

Drown the body in a dam,
Hide it in a garbage can.
Either way that you do,
You'll keep from getting screwed.

Laughter, laughter, all you hear.
Stand on top, live without fear.
Hear the bell, damnation is near,
You'll then cry those soulless tears.
Might take you years.

Hatchet buried deep inside his face,
Crushed all his organs,
Grip the knife and force it to its place,
Now that's a bargain!
Buy it! Buy it! Buy it!

Now that the customer bought your story,
You can be the deacon of the glory.
La la la, la la la.
It can hurt more if you let it affect you,
Or less if you detect the issue.

Now, it takes some time to get over what you've
done,
But rest assured in the end you'll have more fun.
He did you wrong, vengeance is always nice,
And for his family, I'm sure that they'll suffice.

Laughter, laughter, all you hear.
Stand on top, live without fear.
Hear the bell, damnation is near,
You'll then cry those soulless tears.
Might take you years.

Hatchet buried deep inside his face,
Crushed all his organs,
Grip the knife and force it to its place,
Now that's a bargain!
Buy it! Buy it! Buy it!

Now that the customer bought your story,
You can be the deacon of the glory.
La la la, la la la.

It can hurt more if you let it affect you,
Or less if you detect the issue.

I swear on my life,
Didn't mean the knife,
Would drown the flood,
Spill the blood,
All I've done,
Made the cut.
Now you're dead,
Over, over again.

Hatchet buried deep inside his face,
Crushed all his organs,
Grip the knife and force it to its place,
Now that's a bargain!
Buy it! Buy it! Buy it!

Now that the customer bought your story,
You can be the deacon of the glory.
La la la, la la la.
It can hurt more if you let it affect you,
Or less if you detect the issue.

There are no known suspects,
Everyone is to blame.

85.

Golden

My love was alive,
Then I killed it with purpose.
Everyone looked as if I was mad.

I looked in the mirror,
Told myself I'm not worth it.
But I grew to love myself again.

Now I have the next best thing that I believe life
holds,
I don't want to screw it up, living on that isle of lost
marbles.
I have a new life, thanks to a special person.
I know I deserve it.
I know I deserve it.

When you have a fan,
You'll understand,
It's brilliant.
The things that they say to make you alive.

And then the wound,
From the broken glass healed again.
I'm right where I love,
I love where I am.

Maybe the frozen heart turned into fire now,
Maybe that one special fan changed my life now.

Maybe I'm happy because I have found,
A brighter future now.

And I can feel all around,
How he changed my life.
Keep me up, run me 'round,
Gaining back my strife.
Dizzy from,
Hollow moons,
Now I see the light.
Now I see the light.
Golden.

86.

Leave (I Won't Miss You)

I have to tell myself that I'm alright though I'm not,
Because nobody seems to give a shit, and ignoring
the thought,
Of having to listen to someone,
To care for a person who,
Might just be sick and sad enough to be even just like
you.

But it's okay, I'll travel on into my world of self
despair,
I'll thank my friends and family along the way
because those assholes were never there.
So maybe in a sick way this is me thanking you for
everything you've done,
Now please just step aside from my life and let me
move on.

You want me to leave,
And you want to leave me.
Leave me now so I won't miss you when you're gone.
I think that it's hard,
You think that it's easy,
To leave me, you think I won't miss you but you're
wrong.

I said I didn't cut last night,
You I and both know that was a lie,
But the razor is my only companion keeping me
warm and safe and night.
If it wasn't for all the scars and wounds,
You'd be dressed in black and doom,
Watching them lay me into the ground,
Probably hell bound soon.

So, you see my depression is at a lethal state,
My crying spells are negotiable to self despair and
hate.
But I'm saying these words to you now so you
remember them when I'm sane,
Don't ever think I've never wanted sunshine instead
of rain.

And with my head held high I try and better me,
I pick the shattered pieces of my heart upon my
sleeve.
I cry and get the tears out as I can,
Then I focus on our world and find the beauty in a
man.
It's hard when life is such a tragic place,
But you say smile and I get back into my striving face.
And then I fail, but I still try and think of your face.

87.

X Marks The Spot

Where I lay my head.
I set off to sea,
In a desert made just for me.

I jump out,
Of the ship, I play,
In the dried up clay.

Such a nice day awakened to sleep.
Such a nice day to sleep.
I sow, so I shall reap.

What a day for time to collapse,
My ship is sinking, but you'll find the map,
To find my X.
My world is ending, next.
What a day for time to collapse,
My ship is sinking, on a time lapse,
You'll find my X,
My world's at end, world is ending, next.

Let's,
Put on our pirate hats,
And our wear our silly patch,
Find the best in our treasure chest.

'Cause even though,
I maybe fading soon,
There is still some room,
In Davey Jones' Locker of doom.
Such a nice day to sleep.
I sow, so I shall reap.

What a day for time to collapse,
My ship is sinking, but you'll find the map,
To find my X.
My world is ending, next.
What a day for time to collapse,
My ship is sinking, on a time lapse,
You'll find my X,
My world's at end, world is ending, next.

My past life brought me,
Nothing but misery.
Future life will bring,
Smiles and spring flings.

I accept endings,
Endings accept me.
Darker days come before,
Bright days don't just knock on your door...
Knock on your door...

What a day for time to collapse,
My ship is sinking, but you'll find the map,
To find my X.
My world is ending, next.
What a day for time to collapse,
My ship is sinking, on a time lapse,
You'll find my X,
My world's at end, world is ending, next.

What a day for time to collapse,
My ship is sinking, but you'll find the map,
To find my X.
My world is ending, next.
What a day for time to collapse,
My ship is sinking, on a time lapse,
You'll find my X,
My world's at end, world is ending, next.

88.

Good Night

They all look at me like I'm mad,
Maybe I am mad,
It's all I have.
I keep a big secret from you,
And you don't see through,
You think I'm okay, don't you?

I'd hate to be the bearer of bad news, honey,
But I'm so fucking sick that it isn't funny.
My dehydration station is on, water isn't running,
And to you, that means nothing...

What is it I want to satisfy me?
To mend all my broken dreams, fix my crazy?

I'm so broken, so jacked,
I won't ever get back.
So when you say to me that it will be alright,
I just laugh in your face and say I hope you have a
good night.

They say just talk it out,
Well that's a bold statement,
To ever come out of their mouth.
Because they just don't know,
What I had to go,
Through just to stay alive.
They just don't know.

I'd hate to be the bearer of bad news, honey,
But I'm so fucking sick that it isn't funny.
My dehydration station is on, water isn't running,
And to you, that means nothing...

What is it I want to satisfy me?
To mend all my broken dreams, fix my crazy?
I'm so broken, so jacked,
I won't ever get back.
So when you say to me that it will be alright,
I just laugh in your face and say I hope you have a
good night.

Everyone looks upon my Facebook,
Think I want attention,
But did I mention,
I do what I do in spite of what they say.
I do it anyway.

What is it I want to satisfy me?
To mend all my broken dreams, fix my crazy?
I'm so broken, so jacked,
I won't ever get back.
So when you say to me that it will be alright,
I just laugh in your face and say I hope you have a
good night.

My Best Friend, Delilah

My best friend, Delilah,
Knows just how to treat me,
Helps me out completely,
Manages all my pain.

Nobody knows her,
Sinister as always,
Never showing her face,
Because she'll just get judged like I am.

My best friend, Delilah,
You can see my scars.
You can see my sorrow, you can see my heart.
You see through my rear view mirror up ahead,
You can see my ashes in my urn before I'm dead.

Thirsty, keep it coming,
No, I don't need water,
Lila, make it hotter,
I just want to pass out.

I love the feeling,
Delirium stealing,
Catatonic steering,
Just be sure to be on the lookout.

Addiction is hard but self control is harder,
Get the fuck away, I don't want your water.
Drip, drip, drip,
My mind, it slips,
Into a comatose state,
Where I'm catching fireflies and self-hate.

My best friend, Delilah...
My best friend, Delilah...
My best friend, Delilah...
Delilah...
Delilah...

Emotions Are A Bonfire

I scream into the air,
I cry and pull my hair,
I throw my phone across the room,
I laugh at my despair.

I'm a shredded paper,
Scattered in a room.
Looking for a savior,
Someone to take away my gloom.

It works like this,
Emotions are a bonfire.

My scattered ticks,
Are like a golden barbed wire.

I bleed so quick,
My job is now up for hire.

It works like this,
Emotions are a bonfire.

People, they will run,
They will have their fun,
They'll search and destroy you,

Until their job is done.

I'm a shredded paper,
Inside a penthouse.
Haven't found my savior,
All my lights are doused.

It works like this,
Emotions are a bonfire.

My scattered ticks,
Are like a golden barbed wire.

I bleed so quick,
My job is now up for hire.

It works like this,
Emotions are a bonfire.

Emotions are a bonfire...
Emotions are a bonfire...
Emotions are a bonfire...
Emotions are a bonfire...

Turn off all your lights,
Stoop your level down to mine,
Look me into my eyes,
Inside,
Inside, what do you find?
What do you find?
What do you find?

It works like this,

Emotions are a bonfire.

My scattered ticks,
Are like a golden barbed wire.

I bleed so quick,
My job is now up for hire.

It works like this,
Emotions are a bonfire.

91.

Paper Cut

It's written in the sky,
The clouds, they softly cry,
The rain pours down and hides my laughter.
She is ugly, filthy dirt,
But she's my only purpose,
She helps me through my tough times, she shows me
satisfaction.

And it's torture,
It's torture,
What I do to me.
But I really like it,
Can't fight it,
This paper cut.
Paper cut.

My worth is as much as the blade,
Tells me I am,
I can't find another outlet to reside in.
Like slasher films, I'm in one,
I do it to myself,
Am I crazy? Do I need help?

And it's torture,
It's torture,
What I do to me.
But I really like it,
Can't fight it,
This paper cut.
Paper cut.

And it's torture,
It's torture,
What I do to me.
But I really like it,
Can't fight it,
This paper cut.
Paper cut.

Paper cut.

92.

Psycho

Psycho,
Welcome to my world.
It is nice here,
Except when I am disturbed.
Psycho,
Welcome to my world.
Can't dry my frail tears,
Don't you find that absurd?

Happy is the head when the music box is playing,
Dancing when it's dead, all the evil shit they're
saying,
So I drown them out with another song on my
playlist,
Listen to the playlist,
Like a rocker sadist.

Nobody knows quite how to write the pages and just
spill it,
Except for my buddies known as the band Ice Nine
Kills.
Didn't know they had the family quite like they had,

But now they welcome me into their world with open
arms,
(Not bad.

They have no idea how much they mean to me,
My hazardous ways have lead me in disbelief,
That this isn't all too good to be true,
Is it in my head? What should I do...

I'm going underground and these lovely bitches
know it,
And if they have an objection they sure as hell won't
show it,
We stay at sea level, we never sink below it,
I just hope I don't blow it,
Just hope I don't blow it.

They all seem like chill people and I want to just stay
with them,
I want to get to know them better, want to live in
their pen,
I want to love like they love, want to have a new
beginning,
To find a better ending,
A loss from my own winning.

And if you take,
This high away,
Just know one day,
There'll be hell to pay.

93

Thou Art Mine

I'm putting petrifying thoughts up in your head,
I'm gonna make you wish you wish that you were
dead.
I'll never let you go, let you get away,
Your deadly dreams are mine here to stay.

'Cause I am that high pitch,
Crazy witch,
I'm an evil bitch.
You're petrified,
Dead inside,
Nowhere else to hide.

You can't deny,
You're gonna die,

Just go wait inside.
I think I've made up my mind...

I am that wind that blows,
I'm here to chase you.
Got a fear? It shows.
It will embrace you.
And my hungry eyes,
Will never close now,
Thou art mine, beloved, oh thou.

Your dead is better than your single alive,
Your breathing's shallow so I take the dive.
I just can't help myself once I get inside,
I rip your organs then eat them ripe.

Your family comes inside your room the next noon,
They wonder why you never got out of your room.
They look inside your bed find out such a mess,
They yell your name and I wear my dress.

I'm in the rocking chair,
Over there,
With my fancy curls.
Parents shriek,
My winning streak,
I'm a clever girl.
Job is done,
I have won,
Time to run and hide.
But I will see you next time...

94.

Oxygen

I think you're highly mistaken,
Your porcelain's breaking,
I see right through you.
Though my lungs crackle like pop rocks,
I know that you get off,
Everything you do.

Well, you're evil, spiteful, and lie,
You do what it takes in your fucked up mind to make me die.
Can't let you win so I will try,
To wring you like a rag and hang you out to dry.

Sorry to say but pneumonia has died,
I guess I feel sorry but no wait I...lied.

You're always the cold hearted person,
Like Satan among us who lives on this earth.
Your power is greater and worse than,
A demonic savior who plans for his curse.

Can't quite tell if hell's right for you,
You just don't deserve it for all bad that you do.
Die before you kill anyone,
I'll get right to you to make sure that damage is done.

Sorry to say but pneumonia has died,
I guess I feel sorry but no wait I...lied.

I tried telling you that I'm over it,
I just don't care anymore, I don't give a shit.
I've got the antidote, make sure you're prepared,
The light's are now out, now I can breathe air.

Sorry to say but pneumonia has died,
I guess I feel sorry but no wait I...lied.

I should feel sorry now but I can't just... bye.

95.

You Are My Addiction

I am shattered,
Bruised and battered,
Teardrops crack like broken glass.
Watching fire,
Burst desire,
Into flames, I wear my mask.

Pull the needle from the haystack,
It still has thread trailing its tracks.

From what I wear under my skin,
From every breath that I take in,
You are my mistake,
You are lifeless fiction.
No matter how I hide my scars,
There's no denying who you are,
You are my addiction.
You are my addiction.

In my wasteland,
Drop the ink pen,
And I suffer in silence.
Could you give me,
One reason,
To not rid your residence?

And your soulless pool of hatred,
Drowns me in at seven feet.

From what I wear under my skin,
From every breath that I take in,
You are my mistake,
You are lifeless fiction.
No matter how I hide my scars,
There's no denying who you are,
You are my addiction.
You are my addiction.

Hey, don't look back, you are too far gone,
It's time that you move on.
Under attack, there are missiles here,
In the sky, they disappear, it's clear.

From what I wear under my skin,
From every breath that I take in,
You are my mistake,

You are lifeless fiction.
No matter how I hide my scars,
There's no denying who you are,
You are my addiction.
You are my addiction.

You are my addiction.

96.

Here's To You

I haven't been myself here lately,

Everyone's thinking I'm crazy,
They haven't seen a single smile.
When you came riding on your white horse,
It all fell right back on its course,
They don't know you and that's alright.

Because they all say that you're bad for me and I'll
see it in time,
But in all honesty, you're all I have that I can call
mine.

So here's to you, here's to wishing you were true,
But it's okay, darling, we can someday start brand
new.
My thoughts say I love you, self harm, here's to you.
Here's to you, my blade, my best friend, glad it never
did end, oh how I just love the abuse.
My thoughts say I love you, I will always light up that
doused fuse,
I love you, self harm, baby, here's to you.
Here's to you.

Coughing, staying up all night,
Can't breathe because I stopped the fight,
But I kept living all along.
I'm sorry that I took my medicine,
If only I knew now what I knew then,
I wouldn't be here to write this song.

And then the others convince me that I have a
purpose in life,

But I don't deserve the good things that come to their
minds.

I love the way you hurt me, it feels so wrong but feels
so right,
And the fact you were with me on those lonely nights,
When nobody ever saw me cry.

Everyone says you're bad for me,
But you're the one who does adore me,
'Cause when the razor blade hits upon my skin,
Not a thing else in the world matters then.
So I guess in a sick way I've let you win.

97.

Bless This Mind

I hear voices cry as I hang them dry, drown them out
in a river of madness,
They disappear fast, find freedom at last, try to rid
myself of all my sadness.
I scratch for hope on a lottery ticket, dreaming of that
mansion white,
Fields filled with gold, picket fences never ending, oh
it's such my life.

I wasn't moving forward, was only moving back.
My mind it tried to keep all my sanity off track.

Now the morning comes, monsters, your flight is late,
Catch your train, demons, don't hesitate.
Fucking yes, this might just end your fate,
Schizophrenia.

I hated the fact that I was breathing, thought leaving
this world would suffice,
But then in the end, I realized if I'd given in, you
would win every fight.

I wasn't moving forward, was only moving back.
My mind it tried to keep all my sanity off track.

Now the morning comes, monsters, your flight is late,
Catch your train, demons, don't hesitate.
Fucking yes, this might just end your fate,
Schizophrenia.

I just can't please you so I'm gonna leave you instead,
Just go away and yeah that's what I say, leave my
head.
I'll never forget all the endless regrets I'd with you,
Yeah, you've fucked me up, you're so twisted, so
tough, I'm so blue.

Now the morning comes, monsters, your flight is late,
Catch your train, demons, don't hesitate.
Fucking yes, this might just end your fate,

Schizophrenia.

Now the morning comes, monsters, your flight is late,
Catch your train, demons, don't hesitate.
Fucking yes, this might just end your fate,
Schizophrenia.

98.

Leave Me

I have to cover up mirrors to get through the day,
Trying to take showers without them getting in my
way.
Because if I do see in them, I will pick out every flaw,
I will get sick by just staring at the monster that
haunts us all.

I can't stand my unattractive, obnoxious, hollow of a
girl,
I can't stand wanting someone so bad but all they do
is end your end your world.
Every man just seems to run away, seems to leave me
in the dirt,
And everything I've ever wanted in life has lead me
to hurt.

Leave me, go on,
You'll do it anyway.
Leave me,
Don't come running back,
As a matter of fact,
Don't stay.

Leave me, just run,
Run while you still can.
Leave me,
They always do,
You'll see right through,
My ways.

I guess I'm paranoid again, maybe this is all in my
fucked up head,
I think I might have gotten real worse when I wound
up it a stranger's bed.
Four years ago I can't forget, walking down the street
alone,
Then he took me inside and had his way I never
consented, then walked home.

And what about the times when he swore he'd stay,
said he'd pick me up by noon?
I was locked under a trailer full of spiders in a dark
room,
While my sisters were getting taken advantage of
cousins of the Reay's,
But I'd never mention it to their backs or even to
their face.

And now my heart cries and bleeds out my father's
name,
We are closer now than ever, but it will never be the
same.
Because I'm so fucked up from what that family's
done,
It's not his fault for the most part, but my mental
health is on the run.
Alcoholism, kids, it's not so fun to see,
At least it wasn't so fun to witness for me.

And then I grew up only knowing what it's like to
leave...

99.

Shine On, Psychopaths

The girl down the street, they say she is crazy as hell,
Screaming at shadows, tossing tears into a wishing
well.
Wishing she was dead, talking to air, but so sweet,
She says we're all prone to die anyway, might as well
choose defeat.

So maybe crazy is the definition of sanity,
Maybe sanity's the definition of vanity,
Maybe not of us are normal, aren't we?

So if you're crazy, motherfucker, let the world know,
Break all of the normal spectrum barcodes,
And let the psychopathic part of you give a glow.

Shine on, psychopaths.
Shine on, psychopaths.

The girl looked at me, said I don't like it here,
This world is freezing, these people are grinding my
gears.
And even though I try to smile, these people rip apart
my sheets.
She says we're all prone to die anyway, might as well
choose defeat.

So...
Basically, nobody understands.
Everyone tells me to explain.
I can't.
It's hard to talk about your feelings,
When you're a burden.

...Anybody else feel this way?

100.

On The Mend

Hey there, happy, we ended on bad terms,
A smile so dapper, no one knew I was burned.
Love can be so painful, it can hurt so bad,
All of my bleach stains they're drenched in sad.
Tears are falling from what I once did have.

And I had put the blade down,
Finally had enough I was so sick of this town.
And though the chaos did end,
I wanted nothing but to start a new trend.
I just cannot pretend,
I'm on the mend.

Hey there, sadness, I write this letter to you,
Can't help notice you've been feeling down, too.
And I know you really don't like it that way,
You just tell yourself that everyday.
But you hurt me so there's hell to pay.

And I had put the blade down,
Did it with a fragile smile, not a tragic frown.
And though the chaos did end,
I wanted nothing but to start a new trend.
I just cannot pretend,
I'm on the mend.

Thought I found my self control,
Thought my mind was on a roll.

Then my razor became dull,
It was The Battle of the Bulge.
Will I find freedom at last?
Will I set aside my mask?
Will I ever get past,
All of the self hatred I bask.

Don't know the answers, but I'll try my best,
It's deep inside of me, can't escape the rest.
I thought I knew it all, but boy was I wrong,
Never know what you have until it's gone.
So I try,
I fight...

And I had put the blade down,
My circus left without me, ended up the last clown.
And though the chaos did end,
I wanted nothing but to start a new trend.
I just cannot pretend,
I'm on the mend.

I'm on the mend.
I'm on the mend.
I just cannot ever pretend,
I'm on the mend.

About the author:

Karianne Nicole Gabaldon, born and raised in
Arizona and now living her adult years in Hugo,
Oklahoma, decided to write poetry at the age of 13.
She published her very first poetry book, The Crazy
Chronicles, in the year of 2020; along with her first
novella, Crazy, Tortured Souls, which is now a novel.
If you are wondering if Karianne's poems are about
her life, they are 100% about her life. She has
Schizoaffective Bipolar Disorder and Obsessive
Compulsive Symptoms. What is schizoaffective
disorder? Schizoaffective disorder is schizophrenia,
but with another whole subtype. Nobody said having
schizophrenia was easy, but you have to mange to get
by.

Self harm is also discussed here and yes, I'm in
recovery from self harm. It's a day-to-day struggle

but you know how it is. I deeply feel for you if you are a person who has been or is in the same boat, but together we can do it! I also have a therapy cat named Maisy Lynne Gabaldon. Maisy helps with my schizophrenia and syncope episodes. I had a tough upbringing as well, so if any of you struggle with any mental illness, please just know that you're not alone. Everyone gets down, anxious, angry, etc. but it's up to you whether you want to buckle up and face it or not. People often misjudge my reason for writing. This is not a money thing, this is not a fame thing. I write so those who don't have a voice can speak up. Many people in this world are just like, and have, what I'm going through. In the end, we're all the same. So let's put an end to the judging and bullying, let's raise awareness on schizophrenia, and, most importantly, let's give those who can't talk about their problems a voice! I'm fortunate in that department. And let me tell you now, never feel like you're alone. Ever. You matter just as much as the person looking you up and down for the peculiar clothes you have on. Don't you forget it. Thank you all so much for reading! It really warms my heart up knowing that there are people who care.